I0134654

The Book of Youth

Leonid Solovyov

Edited by Doug Frizzle

Stillwoods Edition

Stillwoods.Blogspot.Ca

Catalogue Information:

Title: The Book of Youth
Author: Leonid V. Solovyov (1906-1962)
Edited by: Doug Frizzle (1949-)
ISBN Canada: 978-1-998819-50-8
First published: In Russian 1961; this is first publication in English.
This Edition by: Stillwoods, 2025
ISBN Canada: 978-1-998819-50-8
Blog: Stillwoods.Blogspot.Ca
Storefront: http://www.lulu.com/spotlight/lulubook22

Copyright © Doug Frizzle and/or Stillwoods, 2025.

Keywords: Russia, Tashkent, autobiography

Synopsis: This is a poor translation of a youthful autobiography of the author's life. The author is well recognized for his 'Tales of Hodja Nasreddin' a collection of folklore of Central Asia, where he lived as a youth.

    This novel appears to be autobiographical, but the author is known for his stretching reality.

    The editor apologizes for the quality of this translation and the resulting poor formatting. To reformat a poor translation seemed like making a silk purse…

    I believe the content is important to share with an English audience.   /drf

Contents:

Below is the beginning of the book in Russian:

Леонид Соловьев
Книга юности
Неудачный побег

В тысяча девятьсот двадцать первом году Фергана все еще была одним из центров басмаческого движения. В городах Ферганы и на железных дорогах правили большевики, в сельских местностях — басмачи. Для большевиков борьба осложнялась близостью границ, за которыми сидели англичане, верховные покровители и науськиватели басмачей. Оттуда, из Ирана и Афганистана, шло оружие, прибывали английские офицеры, переодетые в узбекские халаты.

Мы тогда жили на станции Коканд II, в начале железнодорожной ветки, связывающей Коканд с Наманганом. Поезда имели своеобразный вид: впереди шла платформа с уложенными по бортам кипами прессованного хлопка, вперед смотрела трехдюймовка, по бортам торчали пулеметы. За этой укрепленной платформой следовали еще две с рельсами, шпалами, костылями, накладками и прочим путейским хозяйством, затем шел вагон для железнодорожной обслуги, вагон для охраны, потом — собственно поезд, а в хвосте — опять платформа с кипами хлопка и пулеметами. Часто путь оказывался разобранным, рельсы — снятыми и закопанными в песок. Тут же на ходу линию восстанавливали.

На пути к Намангану железная дорога пересекала Сыр-Дарью. Мост был старый, деревянный, раскачанный — его поставили еще до революции, временно, да так и не успели заменить постоянным. Поезд полз по мосту едва-едва, как будто на ощупь, мост скрипел, покачивался, оседал, а внизу, пенясь у деревянных опор, бурлила и клокотала бешеная река, желтая от глины, крученная от водоворотов.

Охраняли мост поочередно кокандский и наманган-ский железнодорожные отряды. Секреты выставлялись далеко по обоим берегам реки и вниз по течению и вверх. Мы, кокандские мальчишки, ездили к мосту на рыбалку. Все другие рыболовные места на магистральных арыках и на озерах вблизи Коканда были нам недоступны из-за басмачей. Основные басмаческие силы держались в горах, но вокруг Коканда непрерывно шныряли мелкие разведывательные отряды и даже часто заходили в старый город, где басмачи имели много сторонников из мулл и бывших торговцев.

Да, в старый город они приходили, и я по ночам иногда слышал далекую стрельбу. А вот к нам в поселок не пришли ни разу. Всякий благоразумный человек только радовался бы этому, но какой четырнадцатилетний мальчишка может быть обвинен в тягчайшем грехе благоразумия? С пылающим сердцем, с неослабевающим нетерпением я ждал, я жаждал, чтобы они пришли! В моем воображении всегда жила пленительная картина ночного боя: вспышки выстрелов, пулеметные очереди, взрывы гранат. И я, и мои две гранаты, и мой подвиг!

About the author:

Leonid Vasilyevich Solovyov (1906-1962) - Russian Soviet writer, screenwriter, author of the dilogy about Hodja Nasreddin (part 1 - "Troublemaker", 1940; part 2 - "The Enchanted Prince", 1954; fully published in 1966).

Leonid Solovyov was born on August 19, 1906 in the city of Tripoli (Lebanon) in the family of an assistant inspector of the northern Syrian schools of the Imperial Orthodox Palestine Society.

In 1909, the family returned to Russia, from where in 1921 they moved to Kokand.

Leonid Solovyov began publishing in 1923 in the newspaper "Turkestanskaya Pravda" (later "Pravda Vostoka") and until 1930 worked as a special correspondent for this newspaper. During his trips to the Fergana region in 1924-1925. L. Solovyov collected and studied folklore. During these years, he recorded songs and tales about V. I. Lenin, which were included in the collection "Lenin and the Works of the Peoples of the East" (1930). According to E. Kalmanovsky, "all the works included there were composed by Solovyov himself, thus creating a folklore and literary hoax."

In 1930, Solovyov came to Moscow and entered the literary and screenwriting department of the Institute of Cinematography, which he graduated from in 1932.

In 1932, his first book-story "Nomadship" was published - about the life of nomads during the years of the revolution, and two years later - a collection of stories and short stories "The Campaign of the "Winner"".

In 1939, the novel "Troublemaker" was published - the first book of L. Solovyov's most significant work - "The Tale of Hodja Nasreddin". In 1935, the film The End of the Half-Station (Mezhrabpomfilm) was shot based on a screenplay by L. Solovyov. In collaboration with V. S. Vitkovich, he wrote the screenplays for the films Nasreddin in Bukhara (1943) and The Adventures of Nasreddin (1946).

During the Great Patriotic War, Solovyov was a war correspondent for the Krasny Flot newspaper. The writer's stories and essays from the front were included in the collections The Big Exam (1943) and The Sevastopol Stone (1944). Based on the story Ivan

Nikulin – Russian Sailor (1943), he created a screenplay for the film of the same name (1944).

In September 1946, Solovyov was arrested on charges of preparing a terrorist act. He was released in June 1954, after spending eight years in the camps. The story "The Enchanted Prince", the second part of "The Tale of Hodja Nasreddin", was written in the camp, based on the script for the film "The Adventures of Nasreddin", and completed by the end of 1950.

From 1954, Solovyov lived in Leningrad. In 1956, "The Tale of Hodja Nasreddin" first appeared in two books in "Lenizdat". The book was a huge success.

Continuing to work in the field of cinematography, Solovyov wrote, in particular, the script for the film "The Overcoat" (1959) based on the story of the same name by N. V. Gogol.

In 1961, parts of L. Solovyov's new work, The Book of Youth, first began to appear in print (a separate edition was published in 1963 under the title From the Book of Youth).

The writer died on April 9, 1962 in Leningrad. He was buried at the Krasnenkoye Cemetery, Narvskaya path.

Bibliography
* Nomad Camp (1932)
* The "Winner's" Campaign (1934)
* Sad and Happy Events in the Life of Mikhail Ozerov (1938) (original title "High Pressure").
* The Troublemaker (1940)
* The Big Exam (1943)
* Ivan Nikulin, Russian Sailor (1943)
* Sevastopol Stone (1944)
* The Enchanted Prince (1954; fully published 1966)
* Sevastopol Stone (1959)
* From the Book of Youth (1963)

Screenplays
* The End of the Stop (1935, co-written with V. Fyodorov)
* Nasreddin in Bukhara (1943, based on the novel The Troublemaker) (co-written with V. Vitkovich)
* The Adventures of Nasreddin (1944, co-written with V. Vitkovich)

* I Am a Black Sea Sailor (1944)
* Ivan Nikulin, Russian Sailor (based on the story of the same name) (1944)
* The Overcoat (based on the story by N. Gogol) (1959)
* Anathema (based on the story of the same name by A. Kuprin) (1960)

Films based on scripts by Leonid Solovyov:
1935 - "The End of the Station"
1943 - "Nasreddin in Bukhara"
1944 - "Ivan Nikulin - Russian Sailor"
1946 - "The Adventures of Nasreddin"
1959 - "The Overcoat"

Failed Escape

In 1921, Fergana was still one of the centers of the Basmachi movement. The Bolsheviks ruled in the cities of Fergana and on the railways, and the Basmachi ruled in the countryside. For the Bolsheviks, the struggle was complicated by the proximity of the borders, behind which sat the British, the supreme protectors and instigators of the Basmachi. From there, from Iran and Afghanistan, weapons were sent, and British officers arrived, dressed in Uzbek robes.

We were living at the Kokand II station at the beginning of the railway line connecting Kokand with Namangan. The trains had a peculiar appearance: in front was a platform with bales of pressed cotton stacked along the sides, a three-inch gun was facing forward, and machine guns were sticking out along the sides. Behind this fortified platform followed two more with rails, sleepers, spikes, pads and other track equipment, then a car for railway service, a car for security, then the train itself, and at the end was another platform with bales of cotton and machine guns. Often the track was dismantled, the rails were removed and buried in the sand. The line was immediately restored on the move.

On the way to Namangan, the railway crossed the Syr Darya. The bridge was old, wooden, swaying - it had been erected before the revolution, temporarily, and they had not yet had time to replace it with a permanent one. The train crawled across the bridge barely, as if by touch, the bridge creaked, swayed, sank, and below, foaming at the wooden supports, the furious river seethed and bubbled, yellow from clay, twisted from whirlpools.

The bridge was guarded by the Kokand and Namangan railway detachments in turns. Secrets were posted far along both banks of the river, both downstream and upstream. We, Kokand boys, went to the bridge to fish. All other fishing spots on the main irrigation ditches and lakes near Kokand were inaccessible to us because of the Basmachi. The main Basmachi forces were in the mountains, but small reconnaissance detachments were constantly scurrying around Kokand and even often went into the old city, where the Basmachi had many supporters from among the mullahs and former traders.

Yes, they came to the old town, and I sometimes heard distant gunfire at night. But they never came to our village. Any reasonable person would have been glad of this, but what fourteen-year-old boy can be accused of the gravest sin of prudence? With a burning heart, with unflagging impatience, I waited, I thirsted for them to come! In my imagination there always lived a captivating picture of a night battle: flashes of gunfire, machine-gun bursts, exploding grenades. And me, and my two grenades, and my feat! I must say that I really did have two hand grenades - bottles that came into my possession ... in a word, the appearance of the grenades in my possession was connected with the distribution of weapons to the soldiers of the railway detachment in the station garden and, in some way, with the insufficient vigilance of the person who carried out this distribution ... but anyway, what is there to go on about - I had two grenades, and that's it!

I kept the grenades under a pillow on the roof of the shed. In Central Asia, it is customary to sleep on roofs in the summer, in the breeze. I arranged my bedroom in the yard on a shed. It was a flimsy structure made of adobe bricks, with a flat roof of reed mats filled with clay. First I climbed the fence, and only then the shed - crawling on my stomach, as if on ice, so as not to fall through. The roof sagged elastically under me and cracked ominously: I was sleeping at the limit of strength.

Our house stood at the very edge of the village. Immediately behind the shed, the fields began, and behind them, in the greenery of the gardens, a small Uzbek village was visible. On the side was an old cemetery overgrown with reeds with Muslim tombstones, from where foxes came to our village to steal chickens. At night, jackals howled and laughed in the cemetery, owls screamed. But I got used to it, and these night voices did not prevent me from sleeping. And an old poplar tree, hanging with its leaves over the shed, protected my sleep from the too-early rays of the sun. And at the head of the bed, under the pillow, lay my two grenades, always loaded, with fuses inserted. "Just in case," I thought. But there was no case, the Basmachi did not come to our village.

They did not go to the village because such a raid was completely senseless. But that did not console me. The main thing was the two grenades; if it were not for the grenades, I would not have been waiting for them so passionately.

And then suddenly Mikhail Kotov appeared in the village, a guy of about eighteen, the son of a road master. He had volunteered in the winter for the Red Army, for the cavalry; now their squadron had been transferred to Kokand, and Kotov had asked his superiors for permission to go home for two days.

He came to the village on horseback, wearing a helmet with a star, with a carbine over his shoulder, and a saber at his side. For two days he was haughtily silent with his peers, smoking, squinting, spitting dryly with some strange, mysterious smile on his face. They expected him to tell stories about campaigns, about skirmishes, but he was silent, and behind this silence everyone imagined extraordinary campaigns and extraordinary skirmishes, so extraordinary that they could not even be talked about, it was forbidden to talk about them. So he rode away on a bay horse, in a foggy cloud of his mysterious glory.

After he left, I fell ill. A little crazy. My two grenades kept coming back to me. So, will they lie there in vain and not bring me any military glory?

One evening my mother, looking at me attentively, asked:

- Are you healthy? Your eyes are shining.

"Quite healthy," I replied. My father said sullenly:

- Yesterday you left a third of the garden unwatered. The tomatoes might wilt. Water them today, and thoroughly. Keep that in mind - I'll check.

I watered the garden, my father checked with a stick how deep the water had penetrated into the soil, and let me go. If only he knew about my plans!

That night before dawn I ran away from home, taking my two grenades. I had prepared a letter to my parents in advance, a short letter and very heartless, as I now understand: "I have left, there is no use looking for me, all the best to you, I kiss you very much..." I went down from the roof of the shed into the yard, the dog Druzhok ran up to me, happily wagging his tail and baring his teeth, smiling with his long, gray, hard-bristled muzzle. It was very early, the birds were still asleep, the sky in the east was just beginning to thaw, there was that special pre-dawn, windless silence that is scary to disturb, it smelled of dewy cool freshness. The windows in the house were open, a dry and hot spirit blew towards me from the room, from the darkness. I put the letter on the windowsill, pressed it down with a piece of brick and left.

I got to the station on a freight train at the brake platform - they didn't take tickets in those years. Karatepa, which is near Andijan, I saw cavalrymen on the platform, asked them where the squadron was. They told me that I was there in half an hour.

I explained to the sentry that I had business with the commander himself. "He's not here, he's gone," the sentry said. "And the commissar?" "The commissar is here, come in."

I found the commissar in the office. He was a short, dark man of about forty, by the name of Nigmatullin, from the Kazan Tatars. He was sitting at a table, reading some paper. I entered, stopped at the threshold, he asked what was going on, and I very coherently told him the legend about myself. There was not a single word of truth in this legend, except for the last name. I called myself a complete orphan, without any relatives on earth, my father, unexpectedly for me, turned into a trackman, killed by Basmachi in the performance of official duties, my mother died of grief - I said it like that: "died of grief", in full accordance with the book by Countess Segur "Poor little devil" - and I ended up as a street child. And now I ask you to accept me into the Red Army, because I want to defend Soviet power with my chest. That's what I said: "to defend with the chest", in accordance with the newspapers and the speeches of the speakers. I don't know what was more in my story - mendacity or an innate inclination to invent, however, it is almost the same thing.

"Where did your father serve, where did he die?" asked the commissar.

- Under the Kermine station. It's beyond Katta-Kurgan, before Bukhara, - I answered without hesitation. - And here... I found it...

And I pulled out my two grenades from the bag, loaded as always, with the fuses inserted. The commissar took the grenades, examined them, and took out the fuses.

- Where did you find them?

- In an empty carriage, when I was coming here. They were lying in the corner.

— So they were lying there with the capsules inserted?

- Yes... That's how they lay.

The commissar put the grenades on the shelf and the detonators in the desk drawer.

- Well, let's go.

4

He took me to one of the long barracks that had survived from the tsarist times and handed me over to the orderly.

- Show him the place.

My place on the bunk turned out to be the last one, right next to the exit.

"Mattress, are you going to stuff the pillow again?" asked the orderly. "No need - he just stuffed them right before the operation."

"Who?" I asked.

- Vanechkin Petr.

- Where is he?

"Killed, buried," the orderly replied and walked away. And from the grey blanket, from the grey mattress without a sheet, from the grey pillow without a pillowcase, it was as if a hot wind of campaigns and sabre fights wafted over me. And damp earth...

I thought that in two or three days they would issue me a uniform, a horse, a rifle and a saber. They issued nothing. The commander still hadn't returned, and the commissar had gone somewhere, and the others didn't care about me. Some stray lad was wandering around the squadron's location, well, let him wander. So I wandered, looking at my feet in embarrassment: the people around me were all wearing boots, because they were cavalrymen, and I was wearing trousers made of devil's leather hanging loose and broken sandals. They fed me, like everyone else, the same millet soup with dried vobla, and didn't ask anything of me. The soldiers looked after the horses, disassembled and wiped the rifles, greased the blades with an oily rag, and I watched all this only from afar.

The squadron was put to rest after a long raid in the mountains, after heavy fighting, the people had not yet recovered, they were still alienated from peaceful life - it is understandable that they hardly noticed me. My neighbor on the bunk was the Cossack from Semirechye Zakharov - a black-haired, pockmarked, high-cheekboned man, unusually incurious. He did not even ask where I was from, what my name was, lay down next to me and immediately fell asleep with a terrible snore.

One day I was the first to speak to him:

— Did you know Vanechkin Petr?

- Of course! - responded Zakharov. - I slept in this very place.

— Where was he buried?

"Near Gulcha," Zakhar answered reluctantly.

— Were you at the funeral?

- Where else would I go? They buried me in front of the line, as always.

— Did you salute?

"What is this?" Zakharov didn't understand.

— Were there fireworks? Rifles fired over the grave?

"Why is that?" asked Zakharov.

- That's how it should be. For the final honor.

- There! - Zakharov grinned. - There won't be enough bullets at this rate, and they all count on a hike, every single one. There's nowhere to take them, what we're carrying with us is all we have. They don't tell us to fire long bursts from the machine gun, only short ones, that's how it is!..

He turned away and began to snore, and I tossed and turned for a long time, experiencing the senselessness of my question, and bitter thoughts came into my head that my affairs in the squadron were not at all as I had thought. But the commissar would return and assign me somewhere, in the most extreme case, even to the office, as an assistant to the squadron clerk.

A day later the commissar returned and indeed assigned me, only not to the office, but to the guardhouse, under arrest.

He brought with him from Andijan a neat little gray-haired old man in a flat straw hat with a black ribbon, a canvas sweatshirt, the same canvas trousers and canvas shoes. Towards evening, when the heat had dropped a little, all the fighters, with the exception of the orderlies, gathered in a clearing in front of a table covered with a red tablecloth.

- Comrade soldiers! - said the commissar. - Comrade professor will now give us a report...

He hesitated, looked at the piece of paper lying on the table, and finished with an effort:

- Selection and mutation... Comrade professor, please. The neat old man stood up, put on his glasses and began in a thin, trembling voice, lisping and whispering:

— Comrades, the issues of selection and mutation have long attracted the attention of scientists from all over the world. American Louis Burbank and our domestic breeder Ivan Michurin from Kozlov…

6

He spoke long and tediously, and all about selection, and mutation was still ahead. The commissar announced a break, the fighters lit up, some ran off to the side behind the bushes, but no one left. The innate delicacy of ordinary people and their reverence for science are great. The fighters sat on the grass and patiently listened to the mutation - stern fighters, who had only just left the battle yesterday, so that tomorrow they would re-enter the battle.

"Any questions for the speaker?" the commissioner asked when the old man finished.

The fighters were silent, coughing discreetly. And suddenly a question was heard:

— When will they give out bread to one and a half juntas?

I recognized the voice of Zakharov, a Semirechye Cossack, my neighbor on the bunk. The old man, apparently not having heard, asked the commissar again. He did not lose his head:

- So, there are no questions. Let's thank comrade professor for the report.

And he clapped his hands. The soldiers clapped in unison. The old man bowed and, accompanied by the commissar, left. They seated him in a green military wagon on forged wheels, and with a rumble in a cloud of dust he left for the station along the dry, broken road, to the train.

And the commissar returned to the clearing, to the table around which the soldiers were crowded, smoking hand-rolled cigarettes.

"What are you saying, Zakharov," the commissar said reproachfully, "what question did you ask him, the professor..."

"But a month and a half ago they said that the junta would be handing out bread," Zakharov replied.

- Understand, chief, this is a matter for the quartermaster, an internal matter, and you should go to a learned man with this.

"That's the point, it's an internal matter," said Zakharov. "With one junta, you can't fight much if you're hungry."

- Then, in such a case, you, Zakharov, should apply to the Basmachi, - said the commissar. - They, the Basmachi, have meat pilaf every day - from rice stolen from the poor oppressed peasants, with lamb, also stolen from the bent poor... And the world proletariat, let it wait until Zakharov has eaten his fill of Basmachi pilaf.

"Don't tell me that, Commissar, don't send me to the Basmachi," Zakharov was offended. "In battle, you know, I'm not behind everyone else."

- I know what you are like in battle, and for your bravery, the workers' and peasants' government thanks you. But your question was very unnecessary. He, the professor, is now riding on a train and thinking about us. What can he think of us after your words, huh?.. They are dissatisfied, he thinks, complaining.

Zakharov remained silent, guiltily looking away. He felt ashamed and walked away. Amazing people stood at the cradle of the new world - wise and naive, merciless and childishly pure. The old man, of course, did not think about anything on the train, and the commissar was worried; not even the slightest shadow would fall on his squadron!

…The commissioner's gaze stopped on me.

- Let's go, let's go. - And he led me to the office. There, in the presence of the squadron clerk, our second conversation took place.

"Sit down, there is no truth in legs," said the commissar. I respectfully sat down on the edge of the lame chair.

The commissioner took off his cap, and a red stripe appeared on his forehead.

- Now tell me again, where was your father serving when he died?

- He served near the Kermine station and died four months ago.

My voice trembled, changed, giving me away completely.

"But from Kermine they responded to my inquiry by telegraph that there is no trackman with that name there and never has been," said the commissioner. "And no one has died in recent years."

The squadron clerk looked up from his writing, a disparaging smile twitching his moustache.

— This is the third time, Comrade Commissar.

- The fourth, - the commissar corrected. - Well, why do they run, why? They need to study, that's why we fight, so that they can study, and here they are!.. And now tell the truth, - he turned to me.

I had to tell. The commissar wrote down the father's name, patronymic, surname, Kokand address, and handed it over to the clerk.

— Notify by telegram. And now send someone here.

About two minutes later, a soldier I didn't know came. "To the guardhouse," the commissar said briefly, and I, accompanied by the soldier, went to the guardhouse - a separate little house with an iron bolt on the door and bars on the windows. Of course, I realized that this wasn't a punishment, but simply a precaution so that I wouldn't run away. But it was still a shame.

Dinner was brought to me at the guardhouse, and half an hour later the Semirechye Cossack Zakharov unexpectedly appeared with a full helmet of large white apricots. He handed them to me through the bars and began a conversation:

I'm telling you this as a bunkmate... But I knew it, brother! - He winked slyly. - I knew it! Our commissar is like that, you can't hide from him. Just like that last fall, one of them showed up to us, just like you. "I'm an orphan, no father, no mother..." You all have the same song. I was angry, but I listened and thought: he's right, there really is only one song.

— The commissar tells him, as if it doesn't matter to you: "I," he says, "sent a request by telegraph..." And what telegraph, he just took it with a cannon, just like he did with you.

He took it "on the gun"! I didn't want to listen to anything else, but Zakharov didn't leave.

— ...His father, you see, was away on a business trip, and his mother came to pick him up. Well, the commissar handed his son over to her, as is proper, and left. And she came to me. "Be so kind," she said, "and teach him properly, like a father, because I have a woman's hand, a weak one." Well, I took off my belt, pulled down his pants, and, you see, I gave him what he deserved...

— They flogged him!

- Of course! - Zakharov exclaimed smugly, striking a spark with a flint on the wick to light a cigarette. - You won't be able to spin around with me, brother! He was screaming so loudly that even the commissar heard him and came running. That was the only way he was saved.

- How do you mean, saved?

- Well, the commissar ordered me to stop, otherwise I would have done more. With me, brother, if you get caught, there's no purr-purr!..

What a man! After all, he was famous throughout the squadron for his bravery, the commissar himself said so today, but he never recalled or talked about battles or dashing sabre fights. But he talked about the boy he had had to flog with the liveliest pleasure, dashingly shaking his black Cossack forelock with gray hair and, apparently, believing that his story gave me the same pleasure.

"So if you had to, you would do it tomorrow too?" I said.

- What of it! - he answered. - You don't need to be spanked, you're no good. But your father will probably come for you. And if it's your mother, then I'll be your father's...

"Executioner!" I thought. "A real executioner!" I was gravely mistaken in my judgment, now it is clear to me that the Semirechye Cossack Zakharov, long torn away from home, while beating someone else's boy, was returning in spirit to peaceful times, to his family, to his fatherly duty - to feed and teach. And that the boy squealed is not surprising, only rare ones do not squeal, and Zakharov's hand was by all indications not very light.

I didn't have to scream, my father came for me. He thanked the commissar very heartfeltly, asked him to come by when he was in Kokand. From his slight accent, he recognized the commissar as a Tatar and became even more fond of him: my father generally had a soft spot for Tatars, Uzbeks, Turkmens, and Kirghiz, considering them people of great honesty and a strong word - in this he was probably not mistaken. The Semirechye Cossack Zakharov shook my hand, and in his eyes, somewhere deep down, I read regret that it was my father who came for me, and not my mother...

I made peace with my father on the train, but my mother was angry with me for longer - she didn't talk. She generally responded to all insults with silence, and this had a depressing effect. My father, for example, couldn't stand her silence for more than two days, and began to fidget and curry favour. Although I shuddered, I held out for three days before I muttered, looking at the ground:

- Forgive me, mom.

Tears came to her eyes, she kissed me and said:

- I didn't sleep at all all these nights while you were gone. Is it possible?..

In the evening, he and my father talked about me in French. They always talked about my sisters in Russian and in calm voices, but as soon as the matter concerned me, they immediately switched to French and changed their voices to raised, nervous ones. This was because the conversation about me invariably turned to some crime. I was definitely a difficult son to raise, my future greatly worried my parents, and they hid their anxiety from me behind the French language. But, surprisingly, I understood everything, although I had never studied French; or rather, I did not understand, but guessed. Here is an approximate summary of their conversation that evening.

"These are the fruits of your influence!" my mother said excitedly. "You are the one who constantly says that a boy should develop courage and independence in himself."

"What do you find wrong with that?" my father objected.

- And the result? He ran away from home!..

- It's okay, madam, every normal boy runs away from home at that age. I ran away too.

- Here you can see bad heredity. Thank God that at least the girls inherited my character and not yours!

...I was on the run for only eight days, and none of my peers would have ever found out anything, but my younger sister Zina let it slip, and everyone found out. Boys are a merciless people, sympathy and delicacy are alien to them, they teased me, hounded me to the end, I could not stick my nose out of the house.

I had to fix things with fights, and I fought skillfully. Not having much strength, I compensated for its lack with agility - for one blow from the enemy I responded with two, maybe not as heavy, but still two and aimed mainly at the "scapula" to "let the juice go". I noticed long ago that "the juice", if let go in time, psychologically weakens the enemy and ensures victory. And when they "let the juice go" to me, I did not pay attention to it - a simple trick, it would seem, but very important in boyish fights.

In the end, my unsuccessful escape was forgotten, and in memory of it I was left with only a new nickname - "Drulya". Why Drulya and what it means, I don't know, maybe it's a derivative of the word "ran away". We, railroad boys, almost never called each other by name, only by nicknames: Kosoy, Pup, Krynchik - these were my comrades, and I myself was Drulya.

I was already entering the age when soon, in a year or a year and a half, I would have to join the clan of our guys and take part in a fierce war with the guys from the railway settlement of Kokand I. This war never stopped, the matured generations gave way on the battlefield to the next older ones. Sometimes the warring clans entered into an alliance to raid the city or, conversely, to repel a raid from their side. And we, fourteen-year-olds, prepared, and quite actively, sometimes opening training military actions against our peers from Kokand I. Here there were ambushes, and encirclements, and capture with subsequent imprisonment in a station toilet, under lock and key, and all sorts of other tricks. I remember Vaska Merkulov, nicknamed Dunya, stole half a box of hunting gunpowder "Bear" from my father, and we began to think about using this gunpowder. Near the depot, in the locomotive cemetery, we picked up a piece of pipe, drilled a touch-off hole in it, and plugged the end of the pipe adjacent to the hole with a babbitt plug. Then we poured all the gunpowder into the pipe, hammered it with a hemp wad, and loaded our gun with medium-sized ramming rubble. Two days later, we started a stone fight with boys from Kokand I; our guys pretended to run and lured the enemy right onto the gun, near which Dunya and I were sitting by the fire with an iron rod stuck in it. When the enemy, victoriously yelling and screaming, approached, I aimed the gun, fixed on a stand made of old bricks, and Dunya pulled a red-hot iron rod out of the fire and stuck it into the touch-off hole. There was an incredible roar, fire splashed into my face, scorching my eyelashes and eyebrows. The enemy ran, and ours rushed after them with screams, shouts, and whoops. The battle was won. Dunya and I examined the burst pipe,

12

the shot hit both ends at once, carried rubble forward, and a babbitt plug back, so far that we couldn't find it...

We spent our time in such not entirely innocent amusements and also in fishing trips to the railway bridge between Kokand and Namangan. And I often thought that I was born at the wrong time - too late to take part in a real war with the Basmachi. I wish I had been born six years earlier, but it turned out to be a shame: the Basmachi are on their own, and I am on my own, and our paths never cross.

But they crossed, and not in jest, but seriously. Further on there will be a story about Katya Smolina, about her father... however, I will start in order, without rushing.

Katya Smolina worked as a registrar at the railway hospital. She was the most beautiful girl in Kokand, which was unanimously acknowledged even by the entire female half of the city. And such recognition, through force, is expensive. She was slender, tall, with a beautiful thin face, with two very long ash-gray braids, I am sure that in any other city she would have been a queen. She behaved accordingly, always a little condescendingly.

Katya had a fiancé, a doctor from the same hospital, Sidorkin. About fifteen years older, acne-prone, always sweaty and shiny, he looked simply ugly next to her, it was insulting to see them together.

Katya's father, Pavel Pavlovich Smolin, worked in a railway office and called himself an old railwayman. In the summer he always wore all white - a cap, a sweatshirt, trousers tucked into light green canvas boots; his face was adorned with a white senatorial beard, combed in two. Only later did it become clear that in fact, in the recent past, he had been a lieutenant colonel in the tsarist army, a Turkestan border officer. Then many things became clear, and, in particular, Katya's previously inexplicable oddities. For example, she shot accurately, went hunting for a semaphore with a double-barreled gun and in boots, rode horseback excellently, and did not recognize ladies' saddles - only Cossack ones. All this ceased to be surprising when we learned that she lost her mother early and was brought up by her father and the Cossacks who made up his border detachment. Katya's father taught her music and French, and the Cossacks taught her shooting and horse riding.

In the summer of 1921, she disappeared from the city, and in the spring of 1922, she was tried by the Fergana Military Tribunal and sentenced to death, with a commutation of ten years in prison. On the way back from the courtroom to prison, she managed to suddenly snatch a revolver from the hands of the senior guard and shot herself in the heart.

Destiny is an internal concept; tragic destinies arise most often from the discrepancy between a person's inner world and the time in which he lives. Katya was at odds with time, her end was predetermined. "Freedom is a conscious necessity" – Katya did not know these words of Engels, and even if she had learned them, she would not have accepted them.

She showed up at our house one summer evening, introduced herself and asked my father for permission to play the school piano in the evenings. And from then on, almost every evening, the captivating sounds of Chopin would come from the open windows of the school. At that time, the only music in the city was performed by a brass band - it is understandable that five or six lovers of fine music would always gather in the front garden under the windows of the school. The concert would end, Katya would come out with her music folder, decorated with a golden image of a lyre and, graciously nodding to the enchanted listeners, would walk away, like a vision, with a light, graceful gait. So amazingly and beautifully, it all went together - the evening, Chopin, her appearance, her gait. And no one knew about the dark depths of her soul.

And there was such a depth. I have already said that the Basmachi had many secret supporters among the traders and mullahs in old Kokand. It turned out that they had secret supporters not only in old Kokand, but also in the railway settlement, the main stronghold of the Kokand Bolsheviks. One day at the end of summer, the three of us: me, Tolya Voskoboinikov and Stepan Pozdnyakov, gathered at the bridge to fish. Tolya and Stepan went to dig worms, and I stayed at home to set up a feeder. It was a dry time, worms were found only along the banks of the irrigation ditches, the largest irrigation ditch closest to the settlement skirted an old Uzbek cemetery overgrown with reeds, and that is where my friends headed.

Half an hour later they returned without worms, but with astonishing news: in one of the collapsed graves at the cemetery, they found six rifles and many zinc boxes with cartridges under the flooring. It should be said here that the Uzbeks buried their dead according to an ancient Muslim custom: they dug a large square room with a deep niche in the wall, put the deceased wrapped in a shroud in the niche, then covered the room with poles, boards, branches and filled it with earth. Over the years, the poles rotted, the grave collapsed. There were many such collapsed graves in the cemetery; in one of them...

After listening, I rushed to the cemetery to see it with my own eyes. Stepan Pozdnyakov, the oldest of us, stopped me.

"They might notice and hide the rifles," he said. "Let's go to Rudakov."

He was an old machinist, a Bolshevik with pre-revolutionary experience, who had been in the Tsar's prison twice, the most respected man in our village. He held some high rank, it seems, the representative of the revolutionary committee for the railway junction.

He was at home. His wife met us in the yard, we said we had important business and were immediately admitted. Rudakov was finishing his dinner, in front of him was a deep plate with tomato and cucumber salad and a thin slice of bread, from which he was taking bites very carefully: bread was in short supply in Kokand at that time and they issued one pound per person per day on ration cards. I remember Rudakov's short-cropped, graying round head and the scar on his forehead - the mark of a Basmachi sabre.

Stepan Pozdnyakov reported, Tolya Voskoboinikov and I only nodded in agreement. Rudakov put down his spoon and did not return for dinner. He asked Stepan in detail where, at what end of the cemetery, the grave was located, made him draw a plan and mark the find with a cross. Then he asked:

- Did you come straight to me? Didn't you tell anyone on the way?

"No," Stepan answered. "We understand."

"Well done!" said Rudakov and took his peeling leather cap off the nail. "Keep quiet, this is a very important matter."

He let us go and went into the city.

"I've gone to the Cheka," Stepan said in a meaningful voice. Tolya and I exchanged glances. "I've gone to the Cheka!.. I hope they don't drag us there too!" A sad feeling arose in my chest that I would definitely end up in that terrible Cheka.

And he got there that same evening. He was the only one of the three who got there, because of his own stupidity. We spent the whole day sitting in our yard, from where the cemetery was visible. We waited for events, perhaps shooting. However, nothing happened. In the twilight, my friends went home, I was left alone. What evil spirit pushed me to go to the cemetery in the semi-darkness, to look at the rifles and ammunition boxes! But I went, found a grave, looked under the collapsed flooring, saw the dull gleaming iron butts of the rifles. I put my hand in, felt the bolt of one. I saw the ammunition boxes too - everything was as Stepan and Tolya had said.

On the way back, almost at our very yard, some stranger caught up with me and put his hand on my shoulder.

"What do you want?" I asked, trying to shake his hand off. It lay there tightly and wouldn't shake off.

"Last name?" he said.

- What do you need it for? - I answered. - Let me go.

"Last name?" he repeated insistently, with a threat in his voice.

I gave my name and showed where I lived. His hand remained on my shoulder.

- Why did you go to the cemetery? What were you doing there? I hesitated: I couldn't just tell him our secret right away. Who knows where he's from, whose, from which side?

"Let's go," he said, squeezing my wrist until it hurt and leading me past the railway line and into the city. A carriage was waiting at a bridge in one of the alleys, we got in and went. He held my hand in the carriage too.

"Are you from the Cheka?" I asked. He didn't answer.

The Cheka was then located on Karl Marx Street.

The carriage drove past the sentry into the yard. In about two minutes we found ourselves inside the building, in a large, spacious corridor with a single door at the end, with two railway-type wooden sofas in front of it. Here my companion handed me over to someone else, and he himself entered the door and closed it tightly behind him. I managed to notice that the door was double, lined on the inside with felt and oilcloth.

The second Chekist who was guarding me was as silent as the first. And I sat and thought about my fate. I can't say that I was particularly frightened: Rudakov was standing behind me.

The first Chekist looked out of the door and signaled me with his finger to come in. I went in and saw Pastukhov himself, the chairman of the Fergana Regional Cheka, sitting at a large desk. He looked at me with an attentive, strangely shining gaze, only later did I realize that his eyes were red-hot from lack of sleep.

"Why did you go to the cemetery?" he asked. "Keep in mind that we only tell the truth."

I had nothing to hide, I told him the pure truth.

"You can ask Anatoly Voskoboinikov and Stepan Pozdnyakov," I finished. "And you can ask Rudakov himself."

"So why the hell did you go to the cemetery?" Pastukhov said, switching to the informal "you". "Why?"

"To look," I answered simply.

- What's there to see! Rifles are rifles, haven't you seen them?

"I didn't realize that you had already put the cemetery under surveillance."

- Why are we sitting here, in your opinion, to catch flies? After all, you could have ruined our operation, and perhaps you already have. Then we will talk differently. Go get Rudakov, - Pastukhov finished, turning to my security officer.

They took me out into the corridor again and handed me over to guards. An hour later they brought Rudakov. I stood up, seeing him, he didn't say anything to me, he just shook his head reproachfully.

Soon I was called to Pastukhov a second time. The office smelled of Rudakov's tobacco - he grew it himself, we boys knew this smell, because we were supplied with tobacco by Rudakov, from his garden, but without his knowledge.

- Well, okay, - said Pastukhov. - It's the first time he says goodbye. So you were going fishing, to the bridge. Why didn't you go?

- Yes, we were late with this matter, we didn't have time to dig up the worms, and the train had already left.

- There will be a train tomorrow at seven in the morning, - said Pastukhov. - So go. And you can dig up some worms on the bridge. In extreme cases, you can catch catfish with raw meat. They catch them, they catch them very well, especially if you stew it a little so that it smells. This is a sure thing, I have caught them this way many times, and successfully.

The telephone hanging on the wall to the side rang. Pastukhov, without getting up from his chair, picked up the receiver. "Yes, I'm listening." He immediately changed, the cheekbones on his face stood out. "Let's bring him to me..." His voice became prickly again, like a Chekist's. He hung up the receiver and looked at me sullenly.

- Don't tell anyone that you were in the Cheka. That's it, go.

We went out, Rudakov and I. In the corridor we met some unshaven man with a pale yellow face, his hands were behind his back. Behind him walked a guard with a revolver in his hand. The door opened silently in front of them and closed again.

In the carriage on the way home Rudakov grumbled at me the whole way, in the end he took pity and shook my hand. He ordered me to wake up Tolya and Stepan early in the morning and be at the train exactly fifteen minutes before departure.

"I'll go with you too, I wanted to do some fishing," said Rudakov. Unaccustomed to lying, especially in front of a boy, he looked off to the side and over my head as he said these words. I immediately understood: he and Pastukhov had decided to remove us from Kokand in such a cunning way. Just in case, it would be calmer. I chuckled to myself, very pleased that I had penetrated their plans. Vanity was mixed in with this: it meant that I was an important person if Rudakov himself was accompanying me on a short and pleasant exile! With complete dignity, I shook his hard hand and left, no longer regretting in the least that I had visited the Cheka.

Rudakov did indeed go with us. By ten o'clock the next day we were on the bridge and immediately went to dig for worms. In the kitchen they gave us a piece of meat, it did not need to be stewed, it smelled pretty good anyway. Contrary to Pastukhov's assertions, the catfish did not take the meat, but they did take the worms briskly. Rudakov did not go fishing with us, making the excuse that he had business to do. When we returned in the evening, we did not find him: he had left on a motorized railcar sent for him from Kokand.

The commander of the bridge guard said that we had to remain on the bridge under his command for three days and not even think about running away with the train. He ordered us to be in his sight every evening when the Kokand train passed.

"Yes," said Tolya, when we left the commander. "Now I understand – they simply kicked us out of Kokand under the guise of fishing."

"They don't trust us," Stepan responded in a gloomy voice. "They're afraid we'll blab. Or we'll go to the cemetery to look. They think we're brats."

I kept silent, blushed deeply and blessed the semi-darkness. He always guessed everything correctly, this Stepan Pozdnyakov, it was as if he was looking into pure water!

Upon returning home, important news awaited us: Pavel Pavlovich Smolin had been arrested. No one in the village understood why.

We crept into the cemetery to the grave - there were no rifles or ammunition boxes. We went to the Smolins' house. The shutters were closed. Katya came out, scooped up some water from the irrigation ditch with a bucket and left again. I never saw her again - she settled in the house and never went out. The hospital hired another registrar to take her place.

Three weeks later, a list of people shot by the Cheka for counter-revolutionary enemy activity was posted around the city. Pavel Pavlovich Smolin was on this list.

And soon Katya disappeared too. At first everyone thought she had been arrested too. Then another rumor came out of nowhere - she had gone to join the Basmachi. Opinions differed, both were probable. They tried to question the doctor Sidorkin, who had been summoned to the Cheka for interrogation (it was known for sure that they had summoned her), but he shrugged his shoulders, made a stupid face and completely denied everything: both the interrogation at the Cheka and his courtship of Katya. His eyes became round, cloudy porcelain, as if sprinkled with powder. I thought of him with contempt: he was afraid of being summoned to the Cheka, big deal!

It was a turbulent time, events were driving each other. People talked less and less about Katya, and by autumn they stopped talking about her altogether.

She reminded us of herself. One autumn night, both railway settlements were raised by the alarming locomotive whistles. "Tu-tu-tu-tu-tu!.." - the locomotives screamed from all the tracks in different voices. The Andreevsky oil mill whistle added its mighty bass to them. There was no fire, so it was a raid. With weapons in their hands, people rushed to the railway hospital.

The Basmachi were not caught. The raid was instantaneous. The Basmachi took the entire pharmacy, all the dressings and surgical instruments, took the doctor on duty, Sidorkin, and galloped away on fast horses.

Katya led the raid. That's how Sidorkin had to meet her, his fiancée...

The Fergana Regional Military Tribunal tried Katya in the building of the railway trade union. The hall was packed with railway workers - engineers, mechanics, switchmen, oilers, turners, blacksmiths... And, of course, their wives. A gloomy day looked through the dusty windows, the faces of the judges, Katya and the guards were unclear, their voices sounded dull. Those in the back kept asking those sitting in front: "What, what are they saying?" The chairman winced, tapped his pencil on the table, demanding silence.

Katya didn't deny anything.

Yes, she went to the Basmachi. Yunus, the assistant of the famous Kurbashi[1] Rakhmankul, came for her with ten horsemen. Late at night there was a knock on the door. She did not yet know who was knocking - the Chekists or the Basmachi. She went up to the door and asked, "Who?" There was no answer. She asked, "Kim?" - and heard the password in response: "Thief." She opened the door, and Yunus stood before her. He led her to the semaphore, to the old brick factory, where the horsemen were waiting. And she left. Yes, there was a free horse for her in the detachment, which was brought by the bridle.

Did she know this Yunus before? Yes, she did – he often visited Lieutenant Colonel Smolin at night. She met him once after her father's arrest, and through Yunus she gave the Basmachi fifteen boxes of rifle cartridges buried in a hole near the bridge on the large Naimanchinskaya road. Her father had whispered about these boxes to her before opening the door to the Chekists. She, however, thought that she would also be arrested, but they left her.

"And in vain, as it turned out," said the chairman. "It would have been better for you yourself if you had been arrested. Then you would not have accumulated so many serious crimes."

"I don't know... Maybe..." Katya shrugged.

The tribunal was particularly interested in fifteen boxes of ammunition. Pavel Pavlovich Smolin apparently had several transfer points for weapons and ammunition. Accordingly, it could be assumed that there were several suppliers. But for now, only one was known - the head of the weapons warehouse in the fortress, and he managed to escape an hour before the arrest.

But Katya didn't know anything about the deliveries. Maybe she didn't want to say anything? No, she just didn't know.

The youngest member of the tribunal, sitting to the right of the chairman, asked:

— Tell me, defendant, was this Yunus your admirer? In love?

---

[1] Kurbashi - here: commander of the Basmachi detachment. — Approx. auto

20

The chairman glanced angrily at him. And Katya answered quite seriously:

- Perhaps. But I had no time for it. Besides, he is Uzbek, and I am a Russian noblewoman.

Her answer left a very unfavorable impression on the court and the public. At that time, people still remembered very well the class and estate strife in pre-revolutionary Russia - "former" people were not liked.

"A former noblewoman," the chairman corrected Katya. She remained silent.

"Ex!" the chairman repeated forcefully. Katya did not respond.

They moved on to other points of the accusation: the raid on the railway hospital, the violent abduction of the doctor Sidorkin, direct participation in the battles. Katya confessed to everything and fell silent, without asking any questions of the witnesses. Only once, when Sidorkin testified that Katya personally shot captured Red Army soldiers, she quietly but clearly said:

- This is not true, why are you lying, Stepan Vasilyevich?!

Sidorkin became embarrassed, began to cough, and his fat, pimply face turned grey.

"Did you see it yourself?" asked the chairman.

"No, I didn't see it myself," answered Sidorkin. "That's what they said."

- Who exactly?

- So... One person... A stranger.

Sidorkin lied out of fear, thinking to flatter the chairman. He could not confirm his words with anything else, and this point of the accusation was dropped.

Katya was captured in battle. The Basmachi gang, of which she was a member, met our detachment in a mountain gorge. The battle ended with the defeat of the Basmachi. Katya's horse was killed, she flew out of the saddle, hit her head on the rocks, and lost consciousness. Otherwise, she would not have been captured alive. Who knows: maybe the bullet fired at her horse was by the Semirechensk Cossack Zakharov?

That same night, the Red detachment raided a Basmachi camp in one of the mountain villages; among others, Sidorkin, who served as the head physician at the Basmachi hospital, was captured there. Previously, the Basmachi entrusted their wounded to the care of tabibs, local healers; only a few recovered; with Katya's arrival, after the raid on the hospital, the Basmachi got a hospital. That's why she needed Sidorkin.

"You seemed to be planning to marry the witness?" asked the chairman.

- No! - Katya laughed openly. - What kind of groom would he be?

Sidorkin turned grey and frowned again.

It later turned out that two captured wounded Red Army soldiers were found in the Basmachi hospital. They were placed in the hospital at Katya's insistence.

"Did Kurbash Rakhmankul himself know about these Red Army soldiers?" asked the chairman.

"Yes, I knew, I even saw them," Katya answered.

"And he agreed to put me in the hospital? That's strange," said the chairman.

"Nothing strange," Katya answered. "A year ago he wouldn't have agreed. But now…"

- What now?

- Now that he has decided to lay down his arms...

"And did he decide so?" the chairman asked quickly.

- Yes. And not only him. Many kurbashis would lay down their arms. They are just afraid of the answer...

"But in our appeals to the Basmachi we guarantee immunity and freedom to all those who voluntarily lay down their arms," said the chairman.

"Yes... However, you are judging me," Katya answered.

- Sorry, you didn't surrender voluntarily. You were captured in combat with weapons in your hands.

"Then I should be considered a prisoner of war," said Katya.

"And the cartridges, fifteen boxes," the chairman reminded.

"Yes, cartridges…" Katya repeated and sat down.

The chairman raised it again.

— What were you guided by when you placed your wounded enemies in the hospital? What considerations? Also about the imminent surrender?

"No," said Katya. "I didn't think of giving up. I was planning to go to Afghanistan. But it didn't work out."

— What were you guided by when placing wounded Red Army soldiers, your enemies, in the hospital?

- Oh, my God! - Katya got angry. - They were wounded! It's quite understandable. A wounded person is sick. He's neither a friend nor an enemy, he's just wounded, and he needs to be treated.

"Yes, now I believe that you did not shoot the prisoners," said the chairman.

"Of course not," Katya answered. "Sidorkin made it all up."

The tribunal gave Katya the last word. She straightened her hair, thought for a moment and said in a calm, even voice:

- I understand that I am wrong. I have long understood that I am wrong. And my father was wrong, I knew that. But I could not do otherwise, I cannot do otherwise now and I will never be able to. Therefore, I ask the military tribunal to shoot me. I have no other choice. And neither do you.

The hall fell silent - no coughing, no whispering, no shuffling of feet. Only Katya's voice could be heard. The tension was becoming unbearable. The chairman could not stand it and angrily interrupted Katya:

— The tribunal itself will decide what sentence to give you.

The audience sighed: Katya would not be shot. And it also became clear that the military tribunal had no intention of shooting her, and the chairman - the formidable, implacable chairman Nikitin! - had conducted the session in this way, so as not to shoot her. Everyone - both the tribunal and the audience - were for this decision, Katya alone was against it.

"You are still very young, you have, oh, so much ahead of you!" the chairman concluded.

"I have nothing ahead of me," Katya answered. The court retired to deliberate.

Half an hour later the sentence was announced: ten years' imprisonment.

I stood in the doorway when Katya was taken out, and I heard the senior guard say to her:

- Don't be so upset. The war will end, there will be a quiet time, and we will let you out. What do we need you for in prison? Live free, we don't mind.

There were three guards, not counting the eldest, and they felt awkward escorting a single girl with such force. The eldest felt awkward too, and he smiled sheepishly, his black moustache twitching. They went down the stairs, the front door slammed, and a few seconds later a shot rang out in the street, unusually loud and distinct. Everyone rushed out into the street, and of course I was the first.

Katya was lying on the pavement, lying with a pale face, with her lips slightly open, with her arms outstretched, pressed tightly to her body.

The escort was at a loss. The eldest, all white, was twirling the revolver in his hands, which Katya had snatched from him a minute before, and muttering incoherently: "How is this possible, huh?.. How is this possible?.." People came running from all sides. A fat switchwoman, Aunt Polya, a well-known Kokand moonshiner, was kneeling over Katya and crying. Then she rose from her knees, wiped her eyes with a handkerchief and said firmly:

- Well, what could she do if she couldn't do it any other way? Such was her fate...

The very next day, a legend spread throughout the city that Katya had actually shot herself because of unhappy love. This legend was, of course, made up by women, but what can you expect from them, from women of that time? In those days, women were different, more naive, more romantic, I would say, and every dramatic event was always explained by unhappy love. But years pass, decades pass, today women have become much more sober, more businesslike.

Two months later, Rakhmankul surrendered. Basmachi in colorful robes rode three abreast across the city square in front of the fortress, and when they drew level with the commander of the Kokand garrison, they piled up their weapons. The old world was leaving, and the winds of new times were blowing ever stronger over the land. And Katya was lying in the cemetery, in the damp earth. Remembering her short but stormy fate now, I think that the fat switchwoman Aunt Polya was right: what else could she, Katya, do if she understood everything, but could not live in a new way?

First Fee

Youth comes to us in different ways: the maturation of the soul, the awakening of passions that have given their voice for the first time. It is a transition to a new world, full of discoveries, temptations and secrets, and each person discovers it anew - the experience of ancestors serves nothing here.

I had just turned seventeen, I was studying at the Kokand railway technical school, and had moved on to my third year. We had our own unwritten rules, according to which students ('listeners', as we proudly called ourselves) starting from their third year were given the right to wear green technical caps with a technical coat of arms: a crossed hammer and a French wrench. The inner spring circle had to be removed from the new cap, then the crown had to be crumpled in a special way in order to give the cap a kind of chic, used look, and only then could it be put on the head. As for the coats of arms, tin ones were sold in small shops, but we preferred silver ones, made to special order. There was an old fat watchmaker on Sovetskaya Street in Kokand who took such orders - and I brought him the silver tablespoon I had stolen from home. The watchmaker was a respectable man, experienced and insightful, and after examining the spoon, he said with a sigh:

- No, young man, take this spoon home and put it back before your mother notices.

I had to attach a dull tin coat of arms to my cap. No matter how hard I tried, cleaning it with chalk and rubbing it with chamois leather, it still remained dull. My listener Zykov, a clever and enterprising guy, came to my rescue - he managed to make silver coats of arms himself and sold them at a considerable profit. Where he got the silver, I don't know, probably also at home from some grandmother's chest.

In a new, luxuriously crumpled cap with a brilliant shining coat of arms, I felt for the first time that I was no longer a boy. At such an age, every little thing has an amazing power over people, like a silver coat of arms, the absence of which can make a person humiliated and unhappy. And youth is very sensitive to the slightest humiliation - that is why in my younger years I so often had to blush hotly and painfully.

...Summer holidays were approaching. These days were marked by unrest in our technical school. The third and fourth years put forward economic demands for special payment for doing homework outside of class at one and a half times the rate, according to the Labor Code (LC). The fact is that according to the rules of that time, our studies were considered work and we were paid not stipends, but wages on par with workers. We thought that they paid little - for this money it was quite enough to just sit in class, and as for homework, well, excuse me, move over.

It is unclear why real workers, genuine fitters, turners, machinists and blacksmiths tolerated such impudence on our part. Even more surprisingly, the railway workers' union supported us. Only the railway management opposed us. We did not achieve overtime (of course!), but a free canteen was organized for us at the technical school. "At least something," we said, and we devoured our lunches regularly, but as before, we did not do our homework, expecting overtime pay.

As I have already said, I had the ability to blush hotly and painfully at any occasion. However, I did not blush when signing the petition for overtime. I blush now, remembering...

With the arrival of summer, football matches began. There were two teams in the city: our "Technical School" and the city "Urak". To tell the truth, "Urak" was stronger, but sometimes, about two matches into the third, ours managed to win.

A brass band always played at the competitions, and goals were scored to the sounds of melancholic waltzes.

This was the case this time: the football players were running, the music was playing, the spectators were whistling, hooting, and cackling – and all of this was being poured down on from above by merciless heat. The sun was roasting the earth furiously, point-blank – the fierce Kokand sun! The sweat on my face dried before I could wipe it off, my face was tight from the thin salt crust.

I was, of course, "rooting" for my team. At first, "Urak" was winning, then the technical school boys won the ball back, the game evened out right before the end, two-two, promising a sure draw.

It was here that an event occurred that turned my whole life around. In the last minute, the left winger of "Urak" sent the ball along our goal. But the goalkeeper of "Tekhnikum" Kelyushenko, who had jumped out in time, caught the ball right in front of the nose of Laktionov, the central striker of "Urak". And before we had time to reward the clever goalkeeper with applause, Laktionov quickly and sharply knocked the ball out of the goalkeeper's hands onto the ground with his hand, and the second striker, Ashot Grigoryan, who was nearby, scored a goal into an empty net.

This lawlessness happened instantly, many spectators did not even notice. The referee was far away and did not notice either. But we, sitting near the gate, saw everything perfectly.

The spectators roared. The Urak fans rejoiced, the Tekhnikum fans were indignant.

But the referee counted the goal, and the final whistle immediately blew.

Following the final whistle, our goalkeeper Kelyushenko punched the center forward Laktionov in the ear.

A fight broke out. They were dragged apart.

The spectators dispersed, the lawless victors proudly left, and only we, the technical school students, remained on the parade ground. What could we do to restore the trampled justice? We could do nothing, we had to be content with the slap that our goalkeeper gave Laktionov.

And yet justice was restored, and I did it.

Returning home late in the evening, I shared my indignation with my family. There was no response: neither my mother, nor my father, nor my sisters were interested in football. I went to sleep on the roof of the shed.

I woke up early, the sun was just rising. I remembered yesterday's football, a hot wave of indignation washed over me again. It was here, on the roof, at this cool and rosy hour of dawn, that a guess struck me: a newspaper!

Where and how this idea came to me is unclear. Until now I had never thought about printing, either jokingly or seriously. I was preparing to be a railway technician, and later, perhaps, with luck, an engineer. But a newspaper, printing!.. Amazing!

At first, lying on the roof, I carefully thought over the article about the lawlessness of "Urak". I recalled all the sins of this team for at least two seasons. When I got off the roof and went to drink tea, the article was already ready in my mind.

It wasn't so easy to put it down on paper. The words were stubborn, confused, repeated and didn't fit together. This was my first warning about the thorns on the path of a writer, but I didn't heed it. And the words continue to torment me to this day - stubborn, confused, repeated and didn't fit together. And nothing can be done about it - such is my fate.

With great difficulty I wrote the article. I reread it aloud and was sadly convinced that it was monstrously long and in no way corresponded in tone or volume to the real significance of the fact. That was how much I understood. But I did not find the strength to rewrite the article. And there was no certainty that the fact itself could interest the newspaper, even if it was described according to all the rules of the newspaper craft.

I signed the article with the pseudonym of The Watcher. It was already four o'clock; the post office would close in an hour. I felt weak and strangely sluggish - from the unaccustomed mental work, as I thought then. Now I know that this was a milestone, the transition from boyhood to youth, and my mysterious hidden self responded to the turn of fate.

Half an hour later it was all over. The receipt for the registered mail was in my pocket. And in the evening I walked and had fun in the city park, completely forgetting about the article and the newspaper.

Five days passed, and the sixth brought me a blow. Luck and a blow at the same time. The article, which had been transformed by someone's skillful pen into a thirty-line note, was printed. And at the bottom there was my pseudonym - "The Awake". True, no more than three phrases from me remained in the note, but the signature was mine.

All that day and the next few I was in a strange, restless and bright stupor of spirit. I kept rereading the note, and it seemed better and better to me. And the main thing was the signature: "The Awake". After all, I am the "Awake". The very fact to which the note was dedicated faded into the shadows, everything was obscured by the signature.

To see my word in print for the first time! I was irretrievably lost to the railway service, a different fate lay before me.

But these were the distant consequences of the note, distant and still unclear. And besides them and independently, there were also immediate consequences.

Kokand was agitated. I mean football Kokand and our technical school. Rumors spread that the Urak team and the referee were writing a joint refutation. Our technical school team urgently, afraid of being late, wrote a confirmation. A mess was brewing. Everyone was asking each other - who is this Awake? Some spoke of him with malice, others - with praise. And I was silent. It was becoming increasingly difficult for me to remain silent. In the end, bursting with vanity, I could not stand it and confessed to my closest friend Tolya Voskoboinikov.

At first Tolya didn't believe it and, blinking his white calf-like eyelashes, said:

- Stop chatting. Someone from Tashkent, from the editorial office, was at the football.

I took Tolya home, showed him the drafts of the article and the receipt from the post office. The receipt said: "Tashkent. Editorial office of Pravda Vostoka." Then Tolya believed me, looked at me with some kind of nasty, drawn-out look and said:

- But if they find out, they'll beat your face in. That's a possibility that never occurred to me!

And when Tolya spoke about her, she immediately stood before me at full height, with all her ruthlessness.

"No one knows except you," I said to Tolya with a hint.

"A grave," he promised.

And I remembered that yesterday I casually bragged about the note to my younger sister. True, she was only twelve years old, but even then she could lisp with her thick tongue to her friends somewhere:

— And my older brother wrote about football players in the newspaper.

I saw Tolya off, found my sister and talked to her for a long time, trying to steer the conversation towards the note with indirect, cunning questions. My sister was flattered by my attention, but she didn't remember about the note. Apparently, she forgot... But when did she forget – maybe after she had already bragged?

I walked away from her with anxiety in my heart. By evening the anxiety had turned into the certainty that my mug would inevitably be beaten.

To this day I still don't know who let me down - my sister or Tolya. I think it was him: he bragged to someone in secret about his friendship with the famous mysterious Watcher. Of course it was him. If my secret had been revealed through my sister, it wouldn't have spread so quickly.

The next morning I was walking along the platform of the Kokand II station and heard the shouts of boys:

- Worker! Rabkor!..

I stopped and looked around. There was no one on the platform, just me and the boys, who continued shouting from afar:

- Worker! Rabkor!..

It happened. Yesterday three knew, today - everyone.

I settled in the railway settlement. Here they couldn't beat me - according to the clan laws, our dashing railway guys would have stood up for me.

Three more days passed. I prudently did not go into the city. But the heavy premonition did not leave me.

I was caught far from the village, at the mill. Here the marinka, the Central Asian ditch trout, was biting well - it was caught on white mulberry berries, letting the line without a sinker on top. Carried away by fishing, I did not notice the approach of the enemies.

There were two of them - Laktionov and Ashot Grigoryan. They cut me off from the shore, and behind me was a deep icy ditch.

"The Awake," Laktionov said ominously. "Let's see now what kind of Awake you are."

I rushed to the side. Ashot Grigoryan intercepted me. He had a dark face, angry eyes, a low forehead - hair grew almost from the bridge of his nose, from his eyebrows. I rushed to the other side, Laktionov tripped me, I fell and covered my head with my hands.

They beat me vilely - with their feet, carefully measuring the force of the blows so as not to cause serious injuries that would be subject to the court's jurisdiction. They beat me for a long time, silently.

- Bathe him! - Ashot Grigoryan suddenly shouted.

"Wait," Laktionov responded. "First, we need to undress you."

They made me strip naked, then lifted me up, swung me and threw me into the middle of the ditch. The fast-moving water, all in foam and black craters, dragged me down. Somewhere below I managed to grab a branch of the coastal willow and climb out of the ditch.

Laktionov and Grigoryan were gone. My clothes and the bucket with the fish I had caught were gone too. The pieces of the fishing rod were lying around.

Wincing in pain, I sat down on a hillock and began to think how I would get home naked now. Should I wait until late at night? Firstly, it would take a long time, and secondly, I would still catch someone's eye at night: the path to the house lay through a large village, there was no bypass road. The appearance of a naked person at night in the village would inevitably cause a terrible commotion and mind-boggling consequences; most likely, the "genies" would consider me crazy, and they would put me in a deep hole, chained to a pole dug into the ground, according to custom. I once happened to see such a crazy person in a distant village - he, covered in wild hair, was sitting in a deep hole and chained to a pole.

The mill turned out to be empty, there was a large padlock on its doors. The harvest had not yet been gathered, there was nothing to grind, the miller was drinking tea somewhere in a teahouse.

There was only one thing left to do: get out to the people, get out to the main road.

I made a circular loincloth from broken willow. In this form I might have been received with friendliness by the Solomon Islanders, but - damn it! - how would the Uzbeks react to my attire?

Along the bank of the ditch, under cover of the bushes, I began to make my way to the main road. Suddenly the path turned and came out of the bushes into a cotton field, open on all sides. Beyond the cotton field, some thickets were visible again. I stood, thought, and with desperate determination went out into the open space.

I went out and ran. How I ran, how I ran! I crashed the bomb into the bushes on the other side of the field and, gasping for breath, fell to the ground.

Having caught his breath, calmed his heart, he listened. The echoes of the highway were already reaching here: the creaking and rattling of carts, the braying of donkeys, the bleating of sheep, the hoarse voices of drivers and drovers.

I crossed another open space just as quickly and found myself in the bushes again - this time close to the road, almost right next to it. But how to get out?..

"Maybe I shouldn't go out in front of dozens of eyes at once," I thought. "It's better to wait here - someone will pass nearby. I'll call this person and tell him my trouble." I spoke Uzbek fluently.

I didn't have to wait long. A group of Uzbek boys of about ten or twelve years old appeared. They came closer. I called out to them in a calm voice. They stopped in bewilderment. I did have a Russian accent, after all, and they caught it.

- Come closer, don't be afraid. I need your help.

They stood still, not moving. And I, invisible, told them from the bushes:

- I lost my clothes and that's why I can't go out to people. I lost my clothes, you see...

No, they didn't understand that. You can lose money, a knife from your belt, or even a skullcap. But how can you lose your clothes?.. Their wariness grew, I felt it.

"Lost his clothes," I repeated. "Look." And stood up before them in all my glory, naked, with a loincloth made of willow.

The boys squealed, "A-a fight!" and scattered. Only the hems of their robes fluttered.

I went cold. They'll bring the adults now. I'm lost! I'm dead! I have to leave. But where? Forward to the road or back to the mill? I decided to go forward, come what may!

And, no longer hiding, I went out onto the country road leading to the large Naimanchinskaya road.

Here, salvation awaited me, a miracle - a bundle of my clothes, tied with a trouser belt. In fact, there was no miracle - my enemies were simply going the same way as me, and, approaching the main road, they abandoned the bundle. Good thing - no one picked it up.

Tearing off my loincloth, I quickly dressed. Just in time - from the direction where I was negotiating with the boys from the bushes, loud voices were heard. The boys brought their fathers and older brothers to my shelter. Now it was not scary - in ten minutes I came out onto the main road into thick fragrant dust.

And immediately the pain returned. All my bones, my whole battered body ached sadly. I arrived home barely alive. I waited in the reeds of the cemetery until evening, slipped into the yard and, gritting my teeth from the pain, somehow climbed onto the shed. I lay down flat and quietly groaned.

My father came out onto the porch and called out to me.

"Yes, here, here," I responded, as if in a sleepy voice.

"Why are you going to bed so early?" said the father. "Who's going to water the garden?"

- I can't today. I'm sick. I'll water tomorrow. Grumbling, rattling the bucket and watering can, my father went to the garden himself. And I spent the whole night in a half-sleep, in a delirious oblivion. I think I had a fever, I had to get down at night to drink from the irrigation ditch. I don't remember how I got down and how I climbed back up the shed.

I had to lie there for three days - a long time for seventeen years. So, I really was beaten badly.

On the fourth day I got up, on the fifth I went to water the garden in the evening and watered it to perfection. Everything went away…

No, it didn't work. There was still a need to pay for the dishonor.

If I had remained a boy at seventeen, I certainly would not have thought of any dishonor. I had suffered before, I was a quarrelsome boy. But the pain passed, and with it the memory of the insult evaporated. Now it did not evaporate, but grew and burned.

I heard the commanding voice of youth, which came to me so unexpectedly and at once. Youth is much more serious than it is usually thought of. I suppose the reason for this is the forgetfulness of adults; however, youth is also forgetful and rarely remembers boyhood. In general, I have often noticed in people and in myself a dull hostility to memories; for some reason, unpleasant events and bad deeds are always remembered, while good ones disappear from memory, as if they belonged not to us, but to someone else.

I decided to talk to my offenders separately in an open and honest fight. Each of them was already over twenty years old, this did not bother me - justice was on my side.

I couldn't talk to Laktionov - he went somewhere far away to Turkmenistan. Ashot Grigoryan, the defendant for both, remained in Kokand.

We met at the city park, in the twilight, on a vacant lot. I appeared in front of Ashot from behind a half-ruined fence. He stopped, his face changing. However, he immediately recovered, seeing that I was alone.

"Ashot, do you know what happens for beating up a worker correspondent?" I said.

"Where are your witnesses?" he answered with an impudent laugh.

I rushed at Ashot. Several times I fell to the ground under the powerful blows of his big hairy fists. I jumped up and rushed again. I did not feel rage, did not scream, did not squeal, but fought with concentration and tenacity. My head was clear, my eyes were tenacious, my fists were fast, the counter-blows did not weaken me. This is what it means to fight when justice and truth are on your side!

Ashot raised his hands, defending himself from a blow to the face, I hit him in the solar plexus, he gave a short yelp, fell down like a sack and never got up again.

I didn't kick him like he did me there at the mill. I immediately cooled down and left. About twenty steps later I looked back.

He was still lying there, raising his head and looking after me, there was redness under his nose. My face was also smashed to the blood, I sat down by the irrigation ditch, washed myself…

This is how I made my debut in print and received my first fee from Laktionov and Ashot Grigoryan.

Talgenism

I loved the old town of Kokand. You would cross the stone bridge over the muddy and shallow icy Sai and immediately find yourself in another world, three centuries back in time. A tangle of narrow streets, blind walls and high clay fences with tightly closed gates; an old man rides on a grey donkey with long ears, his straight legs stretched out in front of him so as not to touch the ground; a woman, wrapped in grey from head to toe, hurries to the pond with a jug in her hands. And the pond, if you come closer to it, is stagnant, covered in green mould, smelling of rot. Antiquity is antiquity, but how could you drink this water?.. That's what I think now, remembering the old days and rejoicing in the new life in Kokand and the new water. But I didn't think like that then; I didn't think at all then, I only saw and heard: I lived by my feelings, and reason was just beginning to flicker in me.

The bazaar is the heart of the old city! It was huge with its squares, horse and cow fairs, a network of covered stalls. Heat, stuffiness, dust, crowds... Sedate merchants with turbans sit motionless in their cramped shops in front of colorful teapots; water carriers, tavern keepers, sellers of snow covered with bekmes, hookah sellers offering everyone a smoke from a hookah for one kopeck, tooth pullers, barbers, fumigators of the sick with the smoke of the sacred herb "khazr-asp", wandering dervishes in conical, fur-lined hats and with black, hollowed-out pumpkins at their belts, shout in shrill voices.

A strange world, an unimaginable mixture of times, sounds, colors and smells! Sometimes I wandered around the bazaar until dusk and left when the lights were already on in the teahouses...

Now, on the site of the bazaar in Kokand, they have laid out a large park of culture and recreation - a shady, cool park with fountains, flower beds and lawns. I did not see a wandering barber, a dervish in a pointed hat, or a beggar disfigured by lupus on its beautiful alleys.

I sat down on a bench and, closing my eyes, tried to imagine the Kokand bazaar. The past arose in my memory vaguely and distantly, and I felt very old, having come from the times of the "Thousand and One Nights". But there are no gray hairs in my head yet: the river of time has so accelerated its flow.

And half an hour later, talking to a group of students from the pedagogical and medical institutes, I felt like their peer in a new life. What an amazing time! Remembering, you feel immeasurably older than your years, turning your gaze to the new - immeasurably younger. And never - in your calendar passport age. This is because the truth of age does not coincide with the calendar.

It was this oldest Kokand bazaar that I decided to describe in my next work for Pravda Vostoka.

The description came to me with unexpected ease, unlike the first article about football. "Wow, things are going well!" I thought, signed myself with the same pseudonym, "Bodstvuyuschiy," and sent the package to the editors.

I waited two weeks, three. The article did not appear in the newspaper. There was no answer. I wrote a letter to the editor, reminding them that I was that very Awake. And again no answer.

And then something indescribable began, very similar to a severe form of graphomania. From morning till night, sometimes even taking up part of the night, I wrote. I composed some absurd fantastic stories, unimaginable stories, even composed poems! Having composed, I rewrote and sent them to many addresses. This continued all summer and all winter and brought the only logical result: in technical school I did not advance from the third to the fourth year, remained a repeater.

At home I said nothing about this catastrophe. "It's still a long way to autumn," I consoled myself, "somehow everything will be sorted out. I can drag out the deception for the winter and confess when I'm already in my fourth year." And I had a brilliant idea of transitioning.

My frantic passion for writing began to subside little by little. Reflecting on my second year, I even recalled my literary experiences with hostility and firmly decided not to return to them. I was faced with a different return - to my former path, to the technical school.

But fate decided otherwise, and I did not return to the technical school. In early June, Tolya Voskoboinikov told me that a scientist had arrived in Kokand from Moscow, who had discovered a new science, "Talgenism." The scientist's last name was Blumkin, and he was accompanied by two assistants. Tolya learned all this from his older brother, the secretary of the factory committee at the cotton gin plant.

The word "Talgenism" meant "talents and geniuses." The Moscow scientist claimed that he had discovered a special, completely infallible method for identifying talents and geniuses from among the masses of the people, especially from among the proletarians. Previously, tsarism had stifled them in the cradle, but now, in the new, Soviet era, they should blossom. Having identified talents and geniuses, the scientist said, it was necessary to conduct a course of studies with them, also using a special method, and in a year to reap the abundant fruits of a new culture, completely proletarian, having nothing in common with the previous, pre-revolutionary culture, the origins of which were rooted in noble-landlord feudalism and in capitalist slavery. "Down with all these noblemen Pushkins, officer-boys Lermontovs, titled landowners Tolstoys and bourgeois-religious neurasthenics Dostoevskys!" the scientist exclaimed in his brochure, published in Moscow by the Proletkult publishing house. The scientist showed leniency only to ancient culture, because Karl Marx himself spoke favorably of it, and everything that followed ancient Greece and ancient Rome was overthrown.

Don't smile ironically, reader. It was the youth of the new world, a great and naive time, a time of enthusiasm and boundless hopes, a time when in the anthem "The Internationale" the words: "This will be the last and decisive battle..." - for the first time, by themselves, were replaced by the words: "This is our last and decisive battle..." They were waiting for a world revolution, waiting for tomorrow, for the day after tomorrow. Victory was won with blood, therefore they affirmed the new and denied the old with fanatical determination, unyieldingly and irreconcilably. Inside the country, everything was being remade in a new way, the "League of Time", "NOT" ("Scientific Organization of Labor"), "daltonplan" and "complex method" in schools, "tests", "psychotechnics", "hyperemotions" appeared. How could a new science "Talgenism" not be born in those years? And she was born... And only in the distant Kremlin, worried captains gathered at night and plotted a course for the ship to the bright shores, foreseeing a dangerous, long voyage in a stormy ocean, which no sailor had ever sailed before.

A day later, the Moscow scientist was supposed to conduct classes with the first group of forty people on the subject of selecting talents and geniuses.

The candidates were sent by the trade unions. I had no chance of being among the forty. That same Tolya Voskoboinikov came to the rescue. I forgot to say that he was the only listener to my stories and tales, and what was most surprising was that he liked them. "Enticing, that's the right word - enticing!" he would say, blinking his calf-like eyelashes. "They must be published, they absolutely must!" Dear Tolya, the only one who believed in my literary calling - he believed in me even when I no longer believed in it myself.

The elder brother arranged for him to be among the forty. Tolya gave me his ticket. At first I refused, I didn't take it.

- And what about you, Tolya?

"What about me?" he smiled. "What kind of talent do I have? I'll just be taking up space."

By the way, he had talent, and a lot of it. Military talent. Tolya began the Great Patriotic War as a lieutenant colonel and ended it as a major general, a division commander. He died three months before the victory - eternal memory to him!

The selection sessions were held in the city trade union club. On the dais for the presidium, sitting at a long table were the chairman of the regional trade union, Kolesnikov, and a Moscow scientist, tall, thin, wearing glasses, with a black beard on a matte yellowish-pale face. I noticed that Kolesnikov was addressing the Moscow guest with some servility, while the latter maintained an imperturbable importance, as befits a person holding other people's destinies in his hands. His assistants, a young man and a young woman, were sitting to the right and sorting through some sheets of paper - "tests", as I learned later.

We, the candidates, were seated at small tables in pairs. I had to sit with Lenochka Pogorelskaya, a well-known beauty in Kokand. Like everyone else, I had long been reverently in love with Lenochka from afar, and she did not even know of my existence. Finding myself in such closeness for the first time, I immediately blushed hotly and began to wipe the sweat from my face with a handkerchief. She was calm and looked through me with her brown eyes, as if she did not even notice me.

Looking around, I saw Vaska Vaganov at the next table - the most desperate fighter and prankster in the entire railway settlement. He winked at me, pointed with his eyes at Lenochka and made an indecent gesture. He didn't even bother to change his clothes and wash up for such an occasion, he came from the depot in what he was wearing - in an oily blouse, barefoot, with oil stains on his forehead and cheeks.

The Moscow scientist tapped his pencil on the table, calling everyone to attention. His assistants, holding stacks of "tests" in their hands, immediately moved along the aisles between the tables. A guy went to the right, a girl to the left.

I saw her close up and was stunned: she was beautiful in both face and figure, like Rachel, Laban's daughter and Jacob's wife, in the Dore engravings from my father's library. She shone with ancient, biblical, noble beauty, and at the sight of her I imagined the white rocky road from Bethel to Ephrath, that is, Bethlehem, where Rachel's tombstone still stands white to this day. And Vaska Vaganov, pointing at her with his eyes, winked at me a second time and made an indecent gesture behind her back a second time.

I turned my gaze to Lenochka. She was also beautiful, but in a different way, in a Ukrainian way. And what good did their beauty do me? And yet I couldn't help but look.

The assistant came up to our table and put a sheet of paper in front of me and Lenochka. These were four phrases, composed in such a way that an absurdity flowed from them; it was necessary to find this absurdity and set it down in writing on the lower half of the sheet.

Lenochka immediately and quite calmly immersed herself in studying the problem, but I couldn't figure anything out. All sorts of things came into my head, but not this problem.

The assistant went to collect the sheets of paper, making some notes in her notebook. I handed her a blank sheet of paper, she looked at me attentively, made a note in her notebook and walked away. After her, a thin spicy scent of perfume remained over the table. Lenochka smelled of perfume too. I realized that I would definitely fail. I had already failed!

We were given another "test" each, I scribbled something with a pencil - I don't remember what. And then the last test began, conducted by the scientist himself. The candidates were called to the table with their heels. The Moscow scientist read some story from ancient times in a measured, dispassionate voice and demanded a conclusion from the subjects. I, Lenochka and Vaska Vaganov were in the third group of five. The scientist read:

— "In ancient Greece there lived a skilled artist sculptor. He carved a marble statue of a woman. She was so beautiful that he fell in love with her and began to beg the gods to bring her to life. The gods heeded his prayers and brought the statue to life. The artist married her. But soon she bored him, and he again indulged in nightly revelry and drunkenness."

At these words the scientist fixed me with a stern, condemning look, as if I were the one indulging in night-time revelry and drunkenness. Then he finished:

"The gods were angry with the artist, and one morning, returning home after a night of revelry, he found a marble statue again instead of his living wife."

After being silent for about half a minute, the scientist pointed his finger at me.

— Conclusion?

- What? - I didn't understand.

"Conclusion?" he repeated. "What conclusion follows from what you have read?"

I had absolutely no idea what conclusion to draw from this story. Shifting from one foot to the other, I said hoarsely:

- Fairy tale…

The scientist exchanged glances with his beautiful assistant. She nodded back, barely noticeable and as if regretfully. He looked at Kolesnikov, the chairman of the regional trade union council, and shrugged. Kolesnikov's face took on a stern, distant expression.

- And your conclusion? - the scientist turned to Lenochka.

"It's the legend of Pygmalion," she said loudly. "The conclusion: with a good attitude towards a woman, you can give life to marble, and with a bad attitude, you can turn a living woman into marble."

The cold importance on the scientist's face was instantly replaced by friendly joy, he smiled and nodded his head. The beautiful assistant nodded and smiled after that, Kolesnikov smiled and said:

- That's right! Under Soviet rule, women have equal rights and husbands shouldn't do such outrageous things.

Lenochka brilliantly passed into the talents. To my surprise, Vaska Vaganov passed too. When asked about the selection, he said:

— We should knock some good drums out for him, this artist, so that he doesn't play around, and put him in the forge at our depot for a couple of months as a hammerman.

"Sly one!" He aimed at the simple working class rudeness and succeeded quite well. The scientist rewarded Vaska with an approving nod.

Only at about six o'clock in the evening the results of the tests were announced. The list of those selected included Lenochka, Vaska and a dozen others. My name was not on the list. Kolesnikov began to talk about the upcoming classes with those selected according to a special program, four hours a day, with two hours allocated from work time at the expense of the regional trade union council, and two hours from personal time. I quietly left.

On the way home lay Kropotkin Park, in the depths of which the mansion of the former Kokand millionaire Knabe gleamed white. I sat down on a bench and sat alone for a long time, until I reached the stars. Something strange was happening inside me, as if the film of my life over the past year was rapidly unwinding in reverse. No, I was not upset that I had not made it into the talents. I should not have gone to the tests. But repeating a year is a serious fact, much more serious than I had initially thought. I decided to confess to my father and mother that very evening - why drag it out?

I was late with my confession.

"Where from?" my father asked in an unkind voice as soon as I entered the room.

Mother sat in a chair in a dark corner and was silent, I did not see her face.

- You stayed for a second year, - said the father. - You stayed and you are cowardly silent. Why didn't you say so right away, straight out?.. No, that's not the main thing. Why did you stay?

I muttered something, as usual in such cases: about the nitpicking and injustice of teachers.

"It's a lie," said father. "I'm a teacher myself and I know all these excuses."

Mother remained silent as before, only sighing in the corner.

"Well," continued father, "then why did you have to repeat a year? Were you forced to work too much at home and had no time for studying?"

This mockery caught my attention.

- Yes, there was no time left. And anyway, I decided to drop out of technical school in the winter.

- What were you thinking of doing?

I had to tell him about writing. My father didn't believe me at first. I took my manuscripts out of the pantry, from under old sacks and mats, and put them on the table. My father was surprised.

- Okay, leave it. Go to bed for now.

I went up to the roof of the shed. From above I saw a lighted open window and my father's silhouette behind the tulle curtain. He was reading my manuscripts. My mother came up and they started talking. About me, of course. I fell asleep, or rather half asleep, anxiously and sensitively. I was awakened by the singing cry of a rooster. The window below was still lit, and my father's silhouette was dark in it behind the tulle curtain.

In the morning he met me serious, reserved and as if he had lost a little weight. And his mother's eyes were red - she had cried at night.

"You're already eighteen years old," said father. "The Germans have a good custom: when a German boy reaches your age and all sorts of fantasies arise in his head, his father sends him away from home for a year. To all four sides, so that this boy can learn about life and try to feed himself."

"But there's only one fourth year left," mother interceded.

Father gently corrected her:

- Not one year, but two - the third and fourth. And the most important thing is that he doesn't want to go back to college. Were you serious about that yesterday?

"Quite seriously," I answered, wanting to appear in my father's eyes as a worthy son, a respectable man who does not change a decision once made.

"As for your writing, I won't take it upon myself to evaluate it," Father continued. "I'm a mathematician, not a teacher of Russian literature. But still, it seems to me that there is something. For example, you write: 'The airship was rushing, carrying a moonbeam on its surface.' That's good, in my opinion – about a moonbeam. But the airship wasn't rushing. These airships are slow-moving. The airship was flying, maybe floating…"

"That's not such a big mistake - in one word," said mother jealously. "And then comes the description of Elizabeth. Her delicate face, framed by golden curls, is very well described.

"I don't argue, I don't argue," answered father. "But we agreed yesterday."

"Yes, we agreed," my mother said in a low voice. I realized that I would have to leave home.

"The German Vater gives his son a knapsack for the journey, in which are placed two towels, a shaving set, two changes of underwear, a spare jacket, trousers and shoes," father continued. "In addition, the Vater gives his son money for the first two months. Are these conditions acceptable to you?"

"Yes, quite," I said. "These are very good conditions."

The next day I left with a knapsack on my back, with sixty rubles in my pocket. My father shook my hand firmly as we parted.

"There are five rubles sewn into the jacket," he warned. "This is emergency money, for a telegram if you get sick or something else happens. But in general, write at least occasionally. We'll expect you in a year."

And he went into the house so as not to disturb my mother as she said goodbye to me. She cried and kissed me.

"The main thing is to be honest always and everywhere," she said. "Here, take this from me."

She put more money in my pocket. I turned and walked away without looking back, feeling her parting glance on my back.

To leave home, to leave home for the first time! An unimaginable expanse opened up before me, a sad, almost evening expanse. Where to go, where and what to look for? It is a very strange feeling when you can take any train in any direction, or even not take a train at all, but walk or ride in a cart... and still...

I stood in line at the ticket office and took a hard ticket with a reserved seat to Samarkand. All the same!..

Kanibadam

Kanibadam is correctly written as "Kend-i-Bodam". "Kend" is "city" in Russian, "Bodam" is "almond", which translates as "Almond City".

Let my poems, written long ago, tell how I came to this poetic city. I have never published poems, but here such a convenient opportunity presents itself, so don't miss it!

Soaking wet, sinking into the clay,
I arrived in Kanibadam in the evening.
March was ending. In the foothills and valley
The rain was already pouring down on the gardens.
The sky was getting dark, night was floating from the east.
The wind died down in the mountains, the sunset faded,
But his trace is on the snowy heights
It was still shining, transparently pinkish.
It was spacious, quiet, empty all around...
And ghostly, like those who are no longer there,
Slightly hovering, misty, inexpressibly sad,
Half-light reflected by the snow.
My path got lost somewhere
In the fields, in the gardens, deserted and naked,
Tears were falling from thin black branches.
About what, about whom? I didn't ask them...
Still without bird songs, without violets,
The gardens listened to the whispers of spring,
Girlishly shy, timid, pitiful,
Full of indescribable freshness,
Not daring to raise my tear-stained eyelashes,
Through such transparent lace,
Turning blue with such airy tenderness,
What is painful to remember and impossible to forget...
Everything was strange, everything was wrong... Visions
Ethereal, weightless, as if in a dream,
And even the sonorous fall of drops,
Perhaps it seemed that way to me?
The mountains were silent, and the gardens were silent,
And only in the distance, in the fog of the damp lowlands,
In selfless sweet sadness

The old muezzin prayed and wept.
What did he sing about, what did he ask God for,
A tired guard and slave of human sins?..
But ahead in the darkness there is already a road
It was marked by the late creaking of carts,
Fences dimly emerged from the darkness,
The smell of dung smoke from the dwelling hit my face...
The gardens ended... The city began here
Kend-i-Bodam, il City of Almonds...

These verses sound somewhat melancholy, but that was exactly the mood I was in at the time. I came to Kanibadam after many fruitless attempts to find any kind of work anywhere. In those years - although this will seem very strange and implausible to today's reader - unemployment was present in the country and was even quite noticeable. "Unemployment was rampant," as they used to say then. In the cities, the unemployed stood patiently for many hours every day in front of the windows of the labor exchanges. They were divided into two categories: "union", that is, members of the union, and "non-union". "Union" members received benefits from the union, and in addition, if they had work, they were the first to be assigned. And "non-union" members received nothing: no benefits, no work.

I was "non-union", in Samarkand my queue at the labor exchange was number 1608, and in the last month only ninety-six people were sent to work, of which only seventeen were "non-union". I realized that there was no point in counting on the labor exchange, I had to look for work myself, and not in big cities, but in villages, far from the railway.

Kanibadam, the district center, although listed as a city, was in fact a large village. Factory and plant chimneys did not rise above its flat roofs, horns did not fill the neighborhood with a cheerful morning call to work. Kanibadam lived by gardens, crafts and trade, lived unhurriedly, in tune with the growth of gardens. The market square was surrounded by a chain of teahouses, there was a covered row and, in addition, many small workshops and shops in the adjoining alleys. It seemed that the entire population of Kanibadam was engaged only in trade and transferred money to each other in a closed ring. But I had nothing to trade with, and I remained outside the ring. What would I do here, how would I live?

I had fourteen rubles and a half left - kopeck for kopeck. And five more untouchable rubles, sewn into my jacket. But I had already gotten used to considering them as non-existent.

I spent my first night in a teahouse: two flatbreads, a bowl of pilaf, a pot of tea, fifty-five kopecks for a night's lodging. I couldn't afford such a large scale, so in the morning I went to look for a place to live for no more than three rubles a month. I walked past the carved walnut gates, knowing that rich people lived behind them, who had no need for three rubles from me, and knocked on the simple wooden gates. And everywhere I heard only women's voices - the men were not at home: they were trading.

But "knock and it will be opened." One of the gates opened, and I saw before me a man of about forty, of average height, slightly reddish, with a beard and moustache. He looked at me sullenly and sleepily. Without any hope of success, I told him my request. He thought about it, scratched his hairy chest.

"Where are you from?" he asked.

"From Kokand," I answered.

— Do you have a father, a mother?

- Yes, I have.

- What does your father do?

"He's a teacher, a domullo," I replied. "We had a little argument, and I left home."

"You can't argue with your father, especially if he's a domullo," my interlocutor said instructively. "That means he's right if he's a domullo. And you just went and left. It's not nice of you, it's disrespectful."

I am citing the entire conversation in detail to emphasize the patriarchal trust and aversion to lies inherent to Uzbeks. "The father of lies is the devil" - they always remembered that. I also tried not to lie unless absolutely necessary, my interlocutor felt the truth in my words with his simple soul.

"Go around the fence," he said. "You'll see a big hole in the fence, come in, I'll meet you."

I walked around the long fence - the house stood on the edge of the vacant lot - saw a gap and went through it into the estate. The owner was waiting for me under the vineyard, there was some kind of building to the side, one half of it was half-ruined, the other was whole, with a window and a door. Further on, there was a fence separating this uninhabited part of the estate from the owner's, residential part.

We looked at the room assigned to me - an ordinary Uzbek room with many shallow niches in the walls for blankets and dishes. The number of blankets in the niches indicated the wealth of the owner. Now the niches were empty due to the absence of the owner; when I rented the room, they remained empty, in accordance with my wealth.

My master's name was Djurabai Alimdzhanov, he served as a district forest ranger - a strange position for a district completely devoid of forests. He received forty rubles a month and for this money he sat out his working hours in the Kanibadam teahouses, because he had nowhere to go and no reason to. But otherwise he was a very good man, kind and oppressed by special family circumstances.

The thing is, he had three wives: the eldest, the middle one, and the youngest, fifteen-year-old Hafiza. I lived alone on my part of the estate, while the owner's part, behind the clay fence, was densely populated. In addition to the three wives, there lived many children from the first two and some old women - relatives in an indefinite number: some disappeared from time to time, others appeared from somewhere. I penetrated into the life that was seething with a stormy spring in the owner's yard with the help of my hearing, through various sounds, mainly women's voices, that reached me. And of course, I did not look through the cracks of the gate or over the fence. But the sounds were quite enough to penetrate. Thus, on the very first day, by evening, I learned that the senior wife of the "baibiche" was a real devil: in such an unbearable shrill voice she cursed her husband, who had let into the house a beggar "kafir"[2], a tramp and a ragamuffin, that is, me. I thanked the Muslim law, according to which she could not appear before me in person. On the second day, I learned - again only by sounds - that the second wife has a phlegmatic, sluggish character and obeys the baibiche in everything, and the third, the youngest, fifteen-year-old Hafiza, is loved and pampered by everyone in the house: both the husband and the senior wives.

This is Hafiza, really very pretty (I saw her by chance once), and was a source of both delight and incessant grief to the master. One evening the sounds in the master's yard began to increase and rise in

---

[2] Kafir (kufr, kafr) is an infidel, that is, one who does not recognize Islam or has forgotten or betrayed its commandments.

tone beyond the usual. At first the shrill voice of the baibiche dominated and covered everything, then I caught the faint sounds of a man's voice coming from the master. Then the voice of the second wife joined in supporting the baibiche, and the master fell silent and was not heard at all. Then suddenly the cries changed to a dull strange noise, in which someone's sniffling and the blows of hard on soft could be distinguished. The noise grew louder, came closer, rolled like a soft puff right up to the fence on the other side, and suddenly the gate swung open with a crash, as if it had burst, and I saw the master.

Having broken through to my part of the yard, he quickly closed the gate and bolted it. Then, forcibly grinning, he came up to me. I noticed a sizeable bump on his forehead, scratches on his cheeks. In addition, he moved his shoulder very suspiciously and stroked his ribs on the left side.

Naturally, I didn't ask him about anything, but ran to the nearest teahouse for tea. When I returned with two teapots and a bowl, the bump on the owner's forehead had already turned purple and was starting to turn dark blue around the edges. We sat down to drink tea, I ran to the teahouse again, and midnight approached. The owner still didn't leave; I realized he was waiting for an invitation to spend the night. I had two blankets, rented from the teahouse and greasy as hell, I gave one to the owner, and we spent the night like brothers on rice straw, without any covering.

During the next two weeks I rarely met the owner and always in passing. He answered my greetings briefly and solemnly, not even turning his head towards me, as befits a respectable man with a home and family, when meeting a homeless tramp who is not driven out of the yard only out of mercy. But once again in the evening, women's voices began to rise in tone behind the fence, and again there was a strange noise, accompanied by the sounds of hard things hitting soft things, and again the owner spent the night with me.

This time he was more talkative.

- Shaitan-baba! Kat-gorichski! - he said. - He himself is an old man, a very old man, and yet he makes noise, shouts!..

These words referred to the baibiche. From the signs on the owner's face it was clear that she was not only "making noise and shouting", but also acting.

From the other side of the fence came unfamiliar female voices, greetings, laughter. The owner listened.

- Mikhmon, you invited guests, a strange woman, you invited neighbors, - he said gloomily. - Oh, the shaitan-woman, completely, completely harmful!..

He finished his tea, filled the bowl again and handed it to me.

- And the young woman Hafiz is a complete idiot, - he continued. - Contemptible... He took a gift, a spirit, poured it on everyone's heads. He sniffs it, everyone knows... Now this, you understand, will be a categorical jan-jal. There will be a scandal!

Here I understood everything. The master, of course, treated his young wife with special tenderness and from time to time brought her gifts from the market - a bottle of cheap perfume or a string of multi-colored beads. The law required that all wives be equally satisfied with the attention of their husbands, including gifts, but three bottles of perfume seemed an exorbitant waste to the master, and he bought one bottle, which he gave to his favorite in secret from the older wives. The fifteen-year-old coquette Hafiz, of course, could not resist and used perfume from the bottle or adorned herself with beads. The secret came to light, and the older wives very energetically reminded the master of their legal rights.

It is curious to note that their anger was never directed at Hafiza, only at the master. And Hafiza remained the favorite of the older wives, who saw her more as a daughter than a rival. During their explanations with the master, Hafiza stood innocently and calmly to the side, looking at him with curiosity with her black, sharp, slightly slanted eyes. And when the master finally escaped to my place, Hafiza passed the bottle to the older wives, and they also put on the perfume. And they invited the neighbors to visit, to show off the gift to them. On the other side of the fence, a mountain of a feast was in full swing, the guests were served dastarkhan, that is, a tray with treats, and the master sat in my room on the straw and, listening to the echoes of the merry feast and gloomily moving his eyebrows, drank thick tea, even without a flatbread.

Thus, I learned some of the peculiarities of Eastern family life, its seamy side, and it became clear to me why the fight against polygamy in the Soviet East did not meet with much resistance from men.

Meanwhile, the time of spring rains had passed, the gardens had dried out and blossomed. Kanibadam was flooded with the white-pink foam of blossoms, the roads were white with petals, the irrigation ditches were becoming fuller and fuller every day, more melodious, the air was fragrant with oil. If only I could, like an ephemeral elf, feed on fragrances! But I was not an elf, but a healthy fellow with a bottomless belly - what to fill it with? I put forty kopecks a day on my food and, of course, I was hungry. In the fall - it was a completely different matter: melons, peaches, grapes! But in the spring, the famous Kanibadam gardens could offer me only fragrance as a gift.

Soon the flowering season ended, the gardens were covered with the finest greenish haze of infant foliage. And with each evening the huge, smoky sunsets over the mountains blazed brighter, more luxuriantly, more passionately; the nights passed, one after another, indescribable smoky-moon nights, and before the new moon - impenetrably dark with a black-transparent and bottomless sky, with huge, living, trembling stars. So I lived that spring in Kanibadam, hungry and delighted.

But there was still no work to be found. The post office did not need a person, the district executive committee conducted its paperwork in the local language, and they did not hire him as a nurse at the outpatient clinic due to the lack of medical training.

Then I turned my gaze to the police. The head of the district police in Kanibadam in those years was Kamil Yarmatov, now a well-lived People's Artist of the USSR, artistic director of the Tashkent film studio. He was tall, and his beauty had a concentrated, introspective, somewhat gloomy character. He appeared in Kanibadam rarely, for a few days, and the rest of the time he spent chasing the remnants of the defeated Basmachi gangs with his detachment of policemen. It is simply amazing that he did not lay down his head somewhere in the mountains.

I approached him one day and asked to serve in the detachment. And was refused. The staff in the militia was also very limited, and besides, special people, properly checked, were accepted for this special service.

I must have looked very pathetic and ashamed during this conversation. Kamil Yarmatov thought, knitting his wide black eyebrows. I didn't even dare to envy him, he looked so magnificent in the tight, creaking belts on his tunic, with a blade on his left side and a Mauser in a wooden holster on his right. And I knew that he didn't wear the blade and Mauser for fashion: only a week ago two of his policemen, killed in battle, were buried.

"Are you well literate?" he asked.

"Yes, good," I answered, wanting to brag about the newspaper article, but holding back.

— Have you seen the long white house near the market? — said Kamil Yarmatov. — There are benches and a stage inside, you can put on different shows. Wait, I'll...

He entered the building of the district executive committee and brought me the key.

- When I get back, I'll raise the issue of a full-time position for the club with the district executive committee. In the meantime, clean things up there.

A policeman-nuker[3] handed him a horse - a grey beauty with dapples, with a bridle decorated with a silver set; Kamil Yarmatov nodded to me and rode out of the gates to the square at a walking pace, to his detachment. And they went off into the mountains, to another operation - the chief in front, followed by two policemen, swaying in their saddles. I watched them go and thought: "Yes, this is a real deal!.." But they left without me.

...The lock on the club door was rusty and wouldn't open. I had to pour kerosene on it. Only after about two hours did the rust soften, come off, and the key turned. Opening both halves of the wide gate-like doors, I entered a long, narrow room. It smelled of warm dust and mustiness, light barely penetrated through the few windows covered in dusty cobwebs, wooden benches stood in two rows, and a platform towered at the end of the room. And I was filled with jubilant joy: all this was mine!

The very next morning I set to work. Wash the windows, sweep the floor, fix the dry, wobbly benches, strengthen the ladder leading to the stage - I managed to do it all in two days. But the walls, the walls - with peeling whitewash, with stains and streaks! I bought chalk and a brush with my own money and spent two more days whitewashing the walls. Having whitewashed, I stayed overnight in the club with the windows and doors open so that it would dry faster.

Now it was possible to show the club to Kamil Yarmatov. But at the district executive committee I learned that he had not yet returned from the operation. The chairman had also gone somewhere, I went to

---

[3] Nuker - a warrior of the ruler's personal guard. Here: orderly.

the secretary of the district executive committee Ishanbaev and respectfully reported to him that the club had been put in order.

This was the same Ishanbaev with whom I would soon have to confront, and not in a figurative sense, but literally. But then I could not foresee such an unexpected turn in my fate. I stood before him and reported and saw from his face that he was hearing about the club for the first time. However, he rose from the table and went with me to have a look.

Never before or since have I met such a disgusting man. His appearance evoked unclean thoughts. His complexion was unusually white, somehow softly creamy, and one could not help but think of the cream compresses with which he undoubtedly moistened his face before going to bed. On this creamy face there was an improbably black moustache with thin ends curled upward, and small, improbably black, sweet eyes sparkled. Under the moustache, his plump lips were tenderly pink, and a blush of the same color shone on his cheeks. He was dressed in a silk robe, tied above his hips, below the waist, with an expensive silk scarf, and he wore narrow patent leather boots with very high, thin heels. And his gait was disgusting, dancing.

He silently walked around the club - my club, with its washed, bright windows, with its repaired benches, with its clean walls, still smelling of fresh whitewash, and just as silently went back to the district executive committee. Not a word, not a sign, not the slightest movement on his face! Having seen him off, I stood at the door of the club in confusion. What did this mean, did he like it or, on the contrary, did he not like it, and what should I expect now?

Later I realized that his silence meant absolutely nothing. He simply saw in this club an unnecessary concern for himself and deflected it in advance - a typical bureaucratic trick.

But the key to the club remained with me, and therefore the position of manager remained.

And I decided to start.

The first performance took place five days later. The athlete Ivan Pavlinov performed. He was truly a man of extraordinary strength. He walked from the station to Kanibadam – ten kilometers away! – carrying a load consisting of two weights, two poods[4] each, a piece of strip iron folded in three, a half-pood sledgehammer on a long handle,

---

[4] A pood is a Russian unit of mass, equal to 16 kilograms (36 pounds). It's a term particularly associated with kettlebell weights in weightlifting contexts.

and a large bucket of water and live frogs. He carried the weights, strip iron, and sledgehammer in a canvas bag on his back, and the bucket in his hands.

The athlete spent the night with me. He was very attentive to his frogs and changed the water in the bucket every two hours.

"What are the frogs for?" I asked.

"For the second section," he answered briefly, continuing to straighten the iron strip with his legs. The athlete was extremely silent.

The following evening, in front of the club, the "karnay" - a long military trumpet - began to roar with an intermittent bass, the pipe began to squeal and the drum began to thunder. The orchestra, hired by me for three rubles, was informing the Kanibadam residents about the performance.

Athlete Ivan Pavlinov demanded some small additions to his inventory - a dozen and a half burnt bricks, a second bucket of water and a large basin. I delivered all this to him and stood at the door, letting the spectators in, charging each one twenty-grivennik.

Very soon the hall was filled to capacity, and the performance began. The first half consisted of exercises with weights. I can testify that these were real two-pood weights, no pretense. The artist worked conscientiously, the muscles bulging lumpily on his arms and legs under his dark skin were real muscles, and the blood rushing to his face from the strain was real blood. He threw the weight high and caught it on his chest or back. I noticed how deftly he squatted to soften the blow. He squatted, but still grunted. Then four hefty spectators, two on each side, bent the iron strip on his neck. The first half of the performance ended with the athlete breaking bricks on his head - that's what he needed the sledgehammer for. When all fifteen bricks were broken, I announced an intermission.

There was no curtain, no wings either, the athlete and I went into a small room adjacent to the stage on the right.

"Are you tired?" I asked sympathetically.

- What's this! - he answered. - The second section is very difficult for me.

With these words he scooped up a large bowl of water from the bucket and drank it. He scooped up a second and drank it. After resting a little, he drank a third bowl and uttered the mysterious words:

- There's no way you can have less than a bucket. Your belly stretches and hurts later. The main thing is that they move and fuss around in your belly, and you have to endure it as best you can.

In about fifteen minutes he drank the whole bucket, his breathing became heavy, a cloudy blueness appeared on his face, and the silver tint on his poorly shaved cheeks became more noticeable.

"Go ahead and announce it," he said.

The second act thrilled both me and the audience. The athlete took a green frog out of a bucket, grabbed it by its hind legs, threw his head back and swallowed it. He held the frog in his mouth for a few seconds to let the audience admire its twitching legs, then swallowed it completely.

The first frog was followed by eleven others. Having swallowed the last one, the athlete walked around the stage several times, slapping his bare stomach with his palms, then bent over the basin and vomited all the frogs out with a fountain of water. The show was over.

That same night the athlete left with his five-pood sack and a bucket of frogs for Isfara, leaving me in grave doubt about the value of the contribution he had made to the young national culture of Kanibadam.

And two days later, another cultural figure stood before me - humorist and satirist Arkady Arkadyev. Again I hired an orchestra, again I collected twenty-grivennik coins at the entrance, and then with bewilderment and a sense of shame I looked at the lively, shabby humorist singing and dancing on the stage. He sang in Russian, the audience did not understand anything, and slowly dispersed. After the concert, Arkady Arkadyev disappeared, taking my new spare trousers and a table mirror from the club. To this day I remember his couplets dedicated to the new American film with Douglas Fairbanks:

From behind the forest, from behind the mountains
The Baghdad thief has arrived;
Don't send us strangers,
We have enough of our own...
I suppose Arkady Arkadyev meant himself...

That was the end of my cultural activities in Kanibadam. Kamil Yarmatov was transferred to another district, I locked the club and handed the key to the district executive committee.

That night, lying on a clay platform under the light of the full moon, I summed up the sad results. The club had given me invaluable experience in dealing with the servants of art, but had brought me no income. It had even taken away the last of my belongings, including my spare trousers. I had enough money for three days, then I would have to rip open my jacket and get out the treasured five roubles. "No way!" I thought. "This five is not for Kanibadam, where I have had such bad luck!" I decided to go even further from the railway, to Ura-Tyube, and try my luck there.

And luck, and rare luck at that, had already come to me and was only waiting for the morning to shine. In the morning I went to a familiar teahouse. The owner, handing me a flatbread and a teapot, said:

- Listen, could you make a sign for me? I'll pay.

"Why do you need a sign?" I asked. "Everyone can see that it's a teahouse."

- They can see, but a sign is still needed, - he sighed. - Yesterday the district executive committee issued an order that all shops, workshops, taverns and teahouses should hang signs. But where can we get them, who will make them? We don't have such a person in Kanibadam.

All the shops, workshops, teahouses and taverns! My head even started spinning!

"And then, they say, there will be a second order to hang a sign on every house: the number, street, and name of the owner," the teahouse owner continued. "It's a real disaster!"

"What a pity," I said. "It's not very easy to write a sign, but I can do it. I had to do it in Kokand."

- Please do it! - the teahouse owner exclaimed joyfully. - And how much will it cost?

"Five rubles," I answered casually. "And if you draw a teapot on the sign, then seven and a half."

I said this price and got scared myself. But the teahouse owner wasn't scared, he just asked just in case:

— Can't it be cheaper?

"It's impossible, that's the tariff," I answered in a seemingly indifferent voice, and he, hearing the unfamiliar word "tariff," meekly agreed and ordered a sign with a teapot. And then he handed me a deposit, two rubles, although I didn't ask for it.

Now it was necessary to act slowly, deliberately. I went to the market square, chose the richest teahouse, where a teapot cost not three but four kopecks, went in and sat down. Here tea was served to the guests by servants - boys, but with a casual movement of my finger I called the owner.

He did not approach me at once. He was important, fat and bearded - a rich teahouse owner, a respectable man, and I was thin, beardless and looked like a boy. But I gave him a second sign with my finger - and he nevertheless approached with a dissatisfied, sleepy look.

"Listen, boss, do you know where I can buy some sheet metal?" I asked. "I can get paint and brushes at the co-op, but I don't think they have any sheet metal there."

He was silent, looking at me with bewilderment, then asked incredulously:

- What, are you into tinsmithing?

"No," I answered. "This is different: the teahouse owner Babajan, who runs a teahouse near the old mosque, ordered a sign from me. If you make it on plywood, it won't last long; you need iron."

"Are you making signs?" the owner exclaimed, and from the tone of his exclamation I understood that there really was an order from the district executive committee.

I immediately accepted the second order and a two-ruble deposit. True, before handing me the deposit, the owner hesitated - was I some kind of rogue, knocking two rubles off gullible simpletons? But luck had already become my kin - among the guests in the teahouse there was a man who knew that I was renting a room for three rubles from the well-known forest ranger Dzhurabai Alimdzhanov. Doubts were removed, and without leaving my place I accepted two more orders - from the tavern keeper and the owner of a shoe shop.

In those NEP years, there were two principles in the country: the growing socialist principle and the dying capitalist principle. And I, having become a lone artisan "without the use of hired labor," occupied a kind of intermediate position between these two principles, like a middle peasant.

April was ending, only the nights with their cool freshness reminded of spring, and the days were already as hot as summer. The oil paint dried quickly in the sun, my work was in full swing.

The customers were generous, and I decorated most of the signs with drawings: for teahouses - a teapot or samovar, for shoe shops - a boot, for hardware stores - a knife. The signs for butchers had no

56

drawing: according to Muslim law, depicting living creatures was strictly prohibited, so I could not draw a ram's or a cow's head. I could not, and would not have been able to - to this day, in the art of drawing, I have not advanced beyond a house. You may ask: how did I manage to depict samovars and boots? I will reveal a secret - with the help of an ABC book and a grid. On the image of a samovar in the ABC book, I applied a thin grid with a pencil, then drew the same grid, but on an enlarged scale, on the sign and transferred the outline of the drawing from the ABC book to the iron square by square. It would have been possible to simplify the matter by using a stencil, but I did not think of it before.

At about three o'clock I finished work, washed, changed clothes and with the signs made yesterday, went to the customers. The rest of the day belonged to me, and I did not know what to do with these evenings. I had no friends, and there was no entertainment in Kanibadam either. My pockets were full of money, but there was nowhere to go. I had never been bored before, absorbed with worries about my daily bread, but now I was bored.

I earned a lot on signs, a lot, about three or four engineering rates. And my sign Eldorado was not in danger of drying up: after all, there was still work ahead to make signs with the name of the street, the house number and the owner's surname. I had already set a price for them in advance - two and a half rubles apiece, and planned to make ten a day. In short, I turned into a typical petty-bourgeois money-grubber. This, of course, was facilitated by my previous lack of money, but still I overstepped my allotted limit. It is embarrassing to admit, but I became stingy in full accordance with the NEP, private capitalist spirit. In the first days of wealth, when I felt the dense bulk of a wallet in my inside breast pocket, and, moving my fingers, in my trouser pockets I pleasantly and smugly felt the sliding coolness of silver, in these first days I generously gave to the poor. Having become accustomed to money, I stopped giving. Truly, being determines consciousness. True, the thought of opening my own shop had not yet occurred to me, but if this continued, it would have definitely come. With each day, with each extra ruble, I grew old in soul and I felt it myself. It is not good when a person with a young face and a slender strong body has a wrinkled soul. Youth does not need a lot of money, it is rich in other things. And extra money takes away youth from a person - in greed and stinginess or in cheap restaurant debauchery, but it definitely takes away.

Love saved me. It was an unsuccessful love, but let it be so! Still, it saved me: it made me leave Kanibadam.

Let us then tell a story about love, about first love. I would get up early, around six o'clock, quickly eat a bowl of sour milk with a flatbread and get to work. I would prepare the sour milk and flatbread the night before and put them on the floor, not far from the slightly open door, in the breeze. I would also sleep on the floor, in the breeze.

One morning I noticed that the top fatty layer of sour milk in the bowl had been licked off. The same thing happened the next morning. Some cheeky cat had taken to visiting me at night, and I decided to teach him a lesson.

I brought a rope from the market (no, not to strangle the impudent cat, my vengeful plans did not go that far) and before going to bed, I tied one end of it to the door and stretched the other to my bed. I closed the window. It was stuffy, I was languishing, but I endured and waited.

The cat came only before dawn. I heard soft, savory licking sounds in the darkness. I quietly pulled the rope, and the door closed. Then, without hiding any more, I stood up, lit the lamp and saw the cat, red, sloppy, with bitten ears, a scratched muzzle and green, bulging eyes.

Have you ever tried to catch someone else's cat with your bare hands in an empty, spacious room? It is an impossible task, beyond human strength. The cat rushed and darted around like a red lightning bolt, bouncing off the walls and jumping to the ceiling, I chased after him and could not catch him. I grabbed a blanket hoping to cover the cat, but I missed and covered the lamp; it tipped over, spilling kerosene on my blanket. Fortunately, it went out before it tipped over, otherwise a fire would have been inevitable. In the ensuing darkness, a small window without glass above the door clearly appeared as a bright square, the cat saw it and darted with a giant leap into this window...

I had to buy a new blanket and throw the old one away - it stank so much of kerosene that it wasn't even good for bedding. "At least he won't come again!" I consoled myself. But a week later the milk was again licked.

I repeated my clever trick with the rope, only this time I boarded up the window above the door with plywood and put the lamp in a safe place.

And the cat was caught! Out of breath, sweaty, with my hands scratched and bitten until they bled, I stuck the cat head down into the top of a canvas boot, leaving only the tail outside. The cat howled and moaned dully in the boot and waved furiously, beating its tail left and right, up and down. "Aha, you don't like it!" I thought vindictively and began the punishment.

In the corner of the room, in the damp sand, I kept a pod of hot red pepper. From the dampness, the pepper swelled and acquired the ability to secrete juice. There is nothing more vicious in the world than this juice! I tore the pod apart and smeared the inside of the wet part under the cat's tail. For a few seconds, the cat was quiet and frozen, as if trying to understand this new sensation for him, then he howled hoarsely and began to twitch in the boot. I went out into the yard, illuminated by the pale, watery-scarlet light of early morning, and shook the cat out of the boot onto the ground.

His eyes were wildly staring, his fur was standing on end. Meowing hoarsely, he jumped onto the roof, from the roof onto a poplar, and back onto the roof. Raising his hind paw, he tried to lick himself, but burned his tongue with pepper juice and screamed at the top of his voice. "I hope I don't die!" I thought anxiously, sincerely feeling sorry for the cat and in my heart reproaching myself for my cruelty. At that moment, a female voice sounded from somewhere above:

- What did you do with my cat?

I looked up and saw a white figure wrapped in a sheet on the roof of the neighboring garden. My neighbor! Until now I knew nothing about her - the entrance to the estate where she lived was from another alley, and we had never met.

"What did you do to him?" she repeated, her voice cold with hostility.

I answered boldly:

- If you keep a cat, you need to feed it.

"My cat is always well fed," she said haughtily. In her answer I heard the unspoken words: "Not like some of the poor tramps of the human race."

"Then why does he lick my milk at night if he's full?" I said and went into the room.

The last thing that reached my ears was:

- Hooligan! Galah!..

My love began with this word "galakh" and ended with the same word. Now it is forgotten, but then it was still in use and meant: "tramp, beggar, beggar, vagabond, idler, drunkard..." What a wealth, what a variety of meanings! Oh, the great, mighty, free Russian language!

Now it is difficult for me to remember how I met and spoke to her; I am sure, however, that this meeting was deliberate on my part. We became acquainted, the adventure with the cat was consigned to oblivion, especially since the cat remained alive and well, but no longer came to my yard. Once I saw him - he was still ragged and sinewy, walking along the ridge of the fence, wagging his tail and turning away contemptuously. I looked at him with penitent tenderness: after all, he was sanctified by her grace and his yellow, bald-spotted, dirty skin was caressed by her hand!

I fell in love, and quickly - it must have been time for me to fall in love. I had no experience in love affairs, I only knew one thing: I was drawn to her with an irresistible force. I don't know whether I behaved stupidly or not, whether my feeling was primitive or sublime - I walked around like a drunk, happily drunk.

She - her name was Tanya - was three years older than me, and ten years more experienced. I was being an idiot in every way possible, and she did not interfere with me. I admit that my selfless boyish adoration was pleasant to her, but nothing more. She immediately understood me to the very bottom and did not even bother to hide her arrogant condescension. To my stupid questions - does she love me? - she answered evasively: "Why else would I get together with you?" I did not remember myself from happiness.

Ten days later she moved in with me. The owner, forest ranger Dzhurabai Alimdzhanov, having learned about this, shook his head understandingly and sympathetically, clicked his tongue and added two rubles a month for the room.

She worked as a telephone operator at the district telephone exchange with twenty-four numbers. I remember the switchboard fixed to the wall; its multi-colored cords with shiny copper tips resembled aiguillettes. And in general, there was something military in the appearance of this switchboard, and in fact it was semi-military. Of its twenty-four numbers, ten belonged to Kanibadam, the rest to the district. The poles carried the wires, squeezing them with porcelain fists, far into the mountains - to Isfara, Chorka and Vorukh, to the restless Basmachi places. Every now and then the telephone connection suddenly broke off; almost always this meant that the Basmachi were preparing another raid and had removed the wire in advance. Armed signalmen came out to restore it. That was where my real place was - among these signalmen, and I was sitting in quiet Kanibadam and writing signs. But I asked to join the police - they didn't take me!

The switchboard was located on the balakhan, that is, on the second floor of a dilapidated house, propped up by pillars; a single-flight staircase led down directly to the street. Here, in the teahouse opposite, I waited for my Tanya when her shift ended. After lunch, we went for a walk to the "waterfalls" — that's what we called one place outside the city, where irrigation ditches converged and then branched out again. The turbid, icy water foamed and made noise on the smooth stones under the huge old willows; the sunset painted it with a transparent scarlet light, like the snow on the distant mountains.

These mountains, the scarlet snows on their peaks! Here, in the valley, night had already reigned, but the snows remained scarlet for a long time and seemed to melt slowly, until only a weak, ghostly half-light remained of them in the sky. I experienced a strange and complex feeling, looking at the fading snows: this was the highest certainty of being, an inseparable fusion with the world and at the same time separateness from the world, my duality - insignificance and greatness, corruption and immortality at the same time. Many times later I saw mountain sunsets, but I never experienced such a clear and precise feeling of my indestructibility in the changing of times. Why? I do not know. Perhaps the source of this feeling was my love? Then I should consider myself lucky on earth, and the love bestowed upon me - the highest blessing. Since then, the naive words: "In you alone is the whole world" - do not make me smile; indeed, the whole world, if without love one cannot feel it as one's own with such certainty. It is common to combine the concepts of "love" and "death" - this is wrong and even blasphemous; the concepts of love and immortality should be combined. But why, I confess, is it given to man to discover the treasures of his soul and rise to the awareness of his immortality necessarily through a woman? Apparently, this is how the world is arranged, and this law is included among its many laws that are incomprehensible to us.

All this was the internal, hidden content of my love and existed only for me, remaining unknown to Tanya. I suspect that Manya or Nadya could have been in her place - I loved for myself, that's the thing. And Tanya knew this - with what kind of woman's intuition, I can't say - and therefore did not take my love seriously. In praise of her, I will say that she did not allow me to spend too much money on her, but she allowed me to be jealous without any restrictions. My stupid jealousy was funny to her, and she sometimes added fuel to the fire with stories about the secretary of the district executive committee Ishanbaev, who was pestering her. Ishanbaev - his creamy face with a glued-on black moustache, his patent leather boots with high thin heels, his depraved, dancing gait! I turned pale and my face turned to stone, hearing this hateful name. And Tanya continued her dangerous game. And in the end, she played herself to the end.

...One day I saw her off to night duty and went to bed early. There was a full moon, a strong blue light illuminated half the room through the open door. The ginger cat came – he now lived with us and even managed to win my respect with his feline prowess – settled down, fidgeted, at my feet and began to purr. I fell asleep.

In the middle of the night I woke up, awakened by a jolt to my heart. I listened - everything was quiet, lizards were chirping in the trees, the irrigation ditch was humming quietly, now growing, now dying away. I was overcome with anxiety: somewhere, something very important to me was happening. A minute later I knew: of course, it was happening to my Tanya, at the telephone station. As if someone whispered to me: "Go, you are needed there..." I jumped up and rushed to the station. One half of the street was black, the other - smoky light blue, the deserted market square seemed huge in the moonlight. And not a soul, as if I was the only one left alive on earth.

I went out to the telephone exchange. The door leading to the balcony was closed with a lattice shutter, the light of a kerosene lamp penetrated into the blue night in yellow stripes. I went up the stairs. Instinct told me that I had to go up very quietly, without noise, without creaking. The second door of the station, leading to the stairs, was slightly open. I looked in and saw Tanya, Ishanbayev in front of her. Tanya was sitting on the table and resting her hand on his chin, and from a distance he was half-embracing her around the waist. My Tanya! Oh, vile rapist! The roles in this fantastic play that I had instantly composed were distributed as follows: a beautiful lady, a vile villain, and a noble, fearless knight who had come to the rescue in time. I burst through the door, Ishanbaev didn't even have time to gasp before he was already rolling down the steep stairs, flashing his embroidered skullcap and high, sharp heels. I'm not sure, however, that he really flashed like that, but that's how I see him now.

Rolling out onto the street, he shouted some kind of threat from below - I remember, he promised to send me out of Kanibadam. I jumped out onto the balcony and threw a flowerpot at him. Ishanbaev jumped back and disappeared into the moonlit darkness. And I, trembling all over, returned to Tanya.

The ending of my fantasy play presupposed words of gratitude through sobs, on the one hand, and courageous consolations, on the other. And I was very surprised to see Tanya's angry, pale face, her cold, hostile eyes.

"What's the matter?" I asked. "Are you unhappy?"

She was silent, her gaze, directed straight at me, became even more hostile.

"What's the matter?" I repeated, feeling my lips curl into an uninvited grin. "Perhaps you made a date with him here, and I interrupted?"

"Galakh!" she said with hatred. "A plucked galakh, that's what you are!" And she burst into tears. These were not the tears of gratitude I had expected, these were completely different tears, born of malice.

- Galakh! - she said through sobs. - What did you think, that I got together with you for good?.. But I only got together with you because there was no one else!.. I need to get married... do you understand, you feeble-minded idiot... get married to a respectable man... so that he would provide for me financially and give me a position... and not to some sign-poster... without a patent...

"I have a patent," I said.

- No, you didn't take out a patent... you didn't take it... I know... you need to be fined a hundred rubles and expelled from Kanibadam!

- I can leave myself, why send me away?

- Well, go away, go away, don't bother me! Maybe I've found my happiness.

- With Ishanbaev? - I grinned. - Well, enjoy it, I won't interfere.
- Galah!

I didn't answer, went down the stairs, and wandered home. It was the first time I had encountered such open betrayal. It was impossible to describe the chaos of my feelings. I knew only one thing for sure: my Kanibadam days were over, I had to leave. And leave immediately, right now, because I wouldn't have the strength to meet her in the morning.

At home I took my knapsack down from the nail. Its buckles had turned yellow and rusty. I packed my underwear, jacket, and trousers into the backpack. Now – the money. I had a little over two hundred rubles in my pocket, and she had hidden the other three hundred and fifty somewhere. I didn't bother looking for it… let it be! It was already getting lighter in the east, and the mountain snows were starting to turn scarlet. And I left Kanibadam.

In the evening I was sitting on the clay bank of the Syr Darya, waiting for the ferry. Kanibadam was visible from here as a light mountain shadow. Again I was free, any road would do for me. My heart was cold, bitter, but pure. The wrinkles disappeared from my soul, but a bleeding scar lay on it. "No matter, this too shall pass," I thought... And since then I have often had to think like this: "This too shall pass…" The ferry was already approaching, two barefoot ferrymen were turning the steering oar with shouts, breaking the current, twisting, furious even here, under the shore. I stood up and went to the pier.

The Intermediate Man

On the other bank of the Syr Darya I walked for a long time, not knowing where, along a well-trodden dusty road, then turned onto a country road. The tracks from the cart wheels were barely noticeable on it, and the horse shoe marks were fresh, people traveled here mostly on horseback. All around was the same crispy porous salt marsh white, dry thorns were yellow, then the country road turned sharply and went deep into the tugai, into wild thickets of low-growing dry-leaved bushes. On the way I came across a channel with green grass along the banks, with a bridge made of poles covered with clay, and with horse shoe marks on the clay. It was already getting dark, in the depths of the thickets pheasants were calling to each other with glassy voices.

I noticed all this with my outer vision and realized it with the surface of my mind, but my soul was still in the night, at the Kanibadam telephone switchboard. And it had to stay there for a long time before I sobered up, came to my senses, and managed to smile at myself for the first time. Worldly wisdom is not cheap for a person in his youth; by the way, it is always a bit akin to cynicism.

Half an hour later I came out of the tight forest into the open. To the right was a chain of dark-brown clay hillocks, behind them a second chain of the same hillocks, higher, a third even higher, and a fourth, and a fifth, like steps rising to the misty-purple Kuramin ridge. And right in front of me stood two small houses of Russian construction. What could this be here, thirty-five kilometers from the railway, in the deserted foothills? Then I saw behind the houses a fenced area with a booth raised on poles, and a ladder in front of it, with a rain gauge and a weather vane. A meteorological observation post, that's what it was!

- Hey-hey! - I called. No one answered. I came closer and called again, and then an old man in a dressing gown, with slippers on his bare feet, with a cataract on his right eye, came out onto the porch from the nearest house. "Hello," I said in Uzbek. He looked me over carefully and went back into the house.

About two minutes later he appeared on the porch again, accompanied by some Russian, unshaven, half-gray, disheveled and dull-eyed. It was clear from the first glance that this man was very drunk.

"Rembrandt, 'Night Patrol,'" he said, smiling vaguely and not noticing my hand extended to him. "Do you remember 'Night Patrol'? You don't remember, you don't know. You're a worm! We're all worms, only worms – you, and me, and that one over there…"

He pointed his finger at the open door behind him, and the old man prayerfully stroked his beard.

- A Muslim, a fatalist, - continued my new acquaintance. - He does not run from his fate. Because of the complete futility of running. What? Did you say something?

I didn't say anything, he just imagined it. The old man took him away and didn't appear for a long time - he was probably putting him to bed. I was sitting on the steps of the porch, a fresh wind blew from the ridge, the tugai darkened, the pheasants fell silent, a night bird gave its first timid call. The silence, the emptiness around suited the emptiness of my soul so well! The old man came out and took care of me - he boiled some tea, gave it a handful of small dried apricots and a stale half-barley cake. That was all I got for dinner, and the old man put me to bed in another empty house, on a trestle bed covered with an old horse blanket smelling of horse sweat. "Where will I spend the night tomorrow?" I thought: the wandering life had begun again.

I slept late, tired from the previous night's walk; when I woke up and left the house, I saw the disheveled drunkard of the previous night heading for the meteorological station. He climbed the steps to the booth and wrote down the thermometer readings in a notebook, then took the soil thermometers out of the ground and wrote them down too. I stood on the porch, waiting for him to return, to thank him for his hospitality and say goodbye.

"Are you ready to go further?" he said in response. "Wait, come with me."

He took me to his little house, and there, in the first room, on a cot, I saw a dead man covered with a sheet. The dead man was very tall, the sheet was missing, and bare legs stuck out from under it, tied above the ankles with an old colored scarf.

"Who is this?" I asked.

"Sergey Petrovich Baryshnikov, or rather what was Sergey Petrovich," my interlocutor answered. "The local meteorological observer. However, he had been ill recently, and I had been acting as meteorologist for him. He died yesterday, an hour before you came to see us."

66

"It's a pity," I said inappropriately.

- Here he is. - My interlocutor lifted the sheet from the dead man's face, I glanced at him and looked away. - Now we'll need your help.

"Please, do you have any shovels?" I said, assuming that he was talking about a grave.

My interlocutor looked at me sideways and, as it seemed to me, mockingly. There was something elusively strange in this conversation near Baryshnikov's body. My interlocutor opened the door to the second room and gestured for me to come in.

This room was larger and brighter than the first, there was an unpainted table, covered with color reproductions of famous paintings, and in the corner a roughly knocked together bookcase showed white. But there were few books, only enough for two shelves. I took one book and opened it - Kuno Fischer, "History of Modern Western Philosophy." On the very bottom shelf lay a stack of ordinary school notebooks.

"Allow me to introduce myself: Ivanov Ivan Ivanovich," said my interlocutor. "In terms of his way of life, he is an intermediate person."

"What do you mean by intermediate?" I asked.

- I'll explain later. I didn't ask for your help to dig a grave, we could have handled that ourselves. But you speak Uzbek, and I don't, and this circumstance makes me turn to you.

He spoke in rounded sentences, emphasizing periods and commas with his voice, as if he were reading from a book. And his face was flabby, puffy, with dark, wrinkled bags under his eyes.

"The late Sergei Petrovich believed in God," he continued. "This should not surprise you."

- I'm not surprised.

- But he was not a religious man. He was a believer, but not religious. Do you understand?

"I don't understand," I said, suspecting that Ivan Ivanovich was still drunk from yesterday.

- He acknowledged the certainty of God's existence and man's involvement with God through the sixth sense - conscience. Personally, I do not believe that we have six senses, not five.

"Okay, okay," I said vaguely. "I'm listening."

- But he believed. And at the same time he did not recognize the truth of any of the existing religions. He considered Mohammed, Christ, Buddha to be just people.

I absolutely could not understand what Ivan Ivanovich wanted from me and what business it was of mine to be concerned with the religious beliefs of the deceased.

- However, before his death, he expressed a wish to be buried according to the ritual. This is exactly what I want to talk to you about.

That he is completely crazy and takes me, a boy, for a priest? The conversation became more and more strange and even fantastic as time went on.

- But how can I help? I don't even know a single prayer to read over the grave.

- Wait, listen to the end. From everything I have said, it is clear that he did not care what the rite was, as long as it was the rite. An Orthodox priest can only be found in Kokand, and it is still unknown whether he will come here. Even if he does come, he will not be here for at least three days, and it is so hot... Do you understand?

He sniffed the air, moving his nostrils, and added mysteriously:

- Already…

I was silent, completely confused. Ivan Ivanovich continued:

- And you can get a mullah. There is a village with a mosque seven kilometers from here. So let the mullah bury him according to the Muslim rite, since the rite is indifferent to him. You know Uzbek, you will go to this village and talk to the mullah...

The fog began to clear before me: this is what Ivan Ivanovich was getting at, it turns out!

I didn't really want to get involved in this Muslim funeral, and on the way to the mosque I thought: "Maybe I should go through the village without stopping and without talking to the mullah." True, my knapsack was left at the meteorological station, but oh well - let it go to waste!.. Well, what if I happen to meet Ivan Ivanovich somewhere later, what will I tell him?

And I still went to the mullah.

He lived near a mosque, in a house with a separate courtyard. All such courtyards are arranged in the same way: in the middle is a hauz, that is, a flowing pond, next to it is a sufa, that is, a clay elevation

68

covered with a carpet, and all this is covered by a thick, impenetrable shadow of an old elm with a round crown.

Lying on the couch, the mullah was enjoying his midday rest. An attendant in a white robe led me to him and stepped aside. I bowed low, to the waist, to appease the mullah, and he nodded casually in response.

- What do you need, Russian?

I explained our case to him. He raised himself on his elbow, the arrogance and sleepiness vanished from his face.

- So, this deceased Russian - may Allah lead him into his heavenly gardens! - came to know the true faith, came to know Islam, before his death?

- I don't know that, he died without me. But the Russian in whose arms he died sent me to you.

"So my words were not in vain," said the mullah. "I thank you, all-merciful and all-powerful, for giving me the power of persuasion."

"Have you ever had to talk to Baryshnikov about faith?" I asked naively.

The mullah whispered a prayer and said sternly:

- Take a rest in the teahouse for now, come here in two hours.

When I came to him a second time, he was no longer alone, he was surrounded by a dozen turbaned old men, some of whom had the end of their turbans tucked up, which indicated that they belonged to the clergy. The mullah made me repeat everything I had told him in private, then with a wave of his hand ordered me to move away. I moved away, but not very much, and heard everything that followed. The turbaned, gray-bearded rogue was lying to the old men with inspiration - he was telling how he had managed to convert the kafir Baryshnikov to Islam and what incredible efforts this pious deed had required. But I knew that there had been no conversion to Islam, that the funeral according to the Muslim rite had been invented by Ivan Ivanovich and only in the absence of an Orthodox priest. I felt like an unwitting accomplice to the roguery that was happening before my eyes, and I could not stop it.

Such blatant fraud, such speculation on a dead man! There was something definitely blasphemous about it. The mullah sent a cart and two servants to the meteorological station for Baryshnikov's body, and I was the third one on the cart.

But when we arrived, there was no one at the meteorological station: neither Ivan Ivanovich, nor the one-eyed old man, nor the dead Baryshnikov. A jackal jumped out of the house right under my feet and ran off into the bushes. A jackal in the house! - that means they've been gone for a long time...

The cart had to be sent back, paying the servants and the driver five rubles for the trouble. I was left all alone between the river and the mountains.

Where did they go, where did they bury the dead man? Maybe another cart turned up and they took the dead man to some other village, where there was also a mosque? But why didn't Ivan Ivanovich leave a note? Was he thinking of returning by evening? Let's wait and see...

There were color reproductions on the table in Baryshnikov's room, and I began to examine them. They were very good reproductions of German work, and on some of them in the upper right-hand corner there was a thin, lightly written pencil note: "Notebook No. Such-and-Such." I leafed through the notebooks, and they contained Baryshnikov's notes on the paintings—philosophical notes that were inaccessible to me at that time. Berkeley, Descartes, Leibniz, Kant, Hegel, Fichte... Of all these names, I had heard only one—Descartes, and that was in the course on analytical geometry that we took at the technical school. "He must be a namesake," I thought, not suspecting the kinship between mathematics and philosophy, and no longer bringing painting and philosophy together in my mind. Meanwhile, Baryshnikov was engaged in precisely the philosophical interpretation of paintings, which is now perfectly clear to me from one of his notebooks that has accidentally survived to this day in my possession. Here are his notes on the Sistine Madonna: Raphael's Sixt. Mad. Modern interpretation: expresses the idea of motherhood, a purely earthly, carnal idea. Superficial and vulgar. Raphael would not have painted such a picture, the idea did not correspond to the spirit of his time.

In the center is the figure of the Woman-Mother, on the sides are two kneeling male figures[5]. What does this kneeling mean, what meaning did the artist put into it?

---

[5] There is a mistake here: the kneeling figures are one male - Pope Sixtus II, the other female - St. Barbara.

Kant: woman in the world expresses the idea of beauty. The judgment of this profound philosopher is astonishing in its hasty superficiality.

In fact, a woman expresses in the world the idea of certainty.

Doubt underlies all classical philosophical systems. From Plato to Hegel, to Mach and Avenarius. Doubt is a purely male trait. It is typical for a man to doubt the evidence of his senses, to disbelieve direct evidence. This is where the Berkeleyan principle, solipsism, was born: only my own existence is certain, everything else is an illusion, just a complex of my sensations.

Theoretically, a man has the right to doubt even the most important thing, his child: is this child really his?

The lot of a man is doubt always and in everything. Hence, from the constant thirst to overcome this doubt, all the wisdom and all the false wisdom of philosophical systems, the creators of which have always been only men. And how can you not turn to philosophy out of grief, if you are not convinced of the truth of the existence of everything that surrounds you?

But women live in certainty. A woman carried and gave birth to a child in agony, try to prove to her by any logic that her child is not really her child and does not exist at all, but is just an illusory complex of her feelings! From the heights of her divinely-certain knowledge, she simply will not listen to you and will not want to delve into it. And if a woman is convinced of the truth of her child's existence, then she is convinced of the truth of everything else that surrounds her.

Women do not compose philosophical systems not because they cannot, but because they do not need to. The world is clear and certain for them, in this sense they are superior to men.

Women do not compose music for the same reason: because music is a philosophy of feelings.

Women are at the same time organically materialistic and organically religious. Materialistic for this earthly, present life, religious for the future. They are much closer to God than men, if He exists, and God reveals Himself to them directly, without any philosophical tricks.

It is precisely this idea of certainty expressed by the Woman that is the idea of the "Sistine Madonna". Hence the kneeling of men and, as the highest proof of the heights of the Woman unattainable for them, the baby in her arms. The baby is male, and look at his face: it is serious, even gloomy and already weighed down with doubt. And the mother looks pitifully at her son, anticipating his male fate, anticipating the prayer for the cup in the Garden of Gethsemane, betrayal and Golgotha..."

I won't hide it: Baryshnikov's notes, reread recently, seemed to me much more interesting than those meager ideas, set out both in prose and in verse, where Raphael's Madonna is still interpreted as simply a mother-nurse and with a bias towards an atheistic meaning. Too free an approach to the era, I think. But that's what I think now, but then, when I first saw these notes, I didn't understand anything in them, and I didn't try to understand, being busy with other thoughts - about the mysterious disappearance of two living and one dead person.

I found myself in a strange situation, a very strange one. Leave, like them? But the devices, the books, the reproductions. How can I leave all this, I have to give it to someone. But to whom? There are birds and animals all around. Stay? What if there is a murder here, then go and prove your innocence.

Again, before evening, pheasants called to each other with glassy voices in the tugai[6], again an indescribable, passionately crimson sunset blazed over the Kuramin ridge, again night came, bats traced lines in the sky, night sounds were heard from the tugai - crackling in the thicket and splashing in the water: wild boars rose from their daytime beds.

That night I climbed onto the roof to sleep: the devil knows, maybe some stray leopard got stuck in the thicket, the mountains are nearby. Or maybe those two who disappeared might show up at night. I dragged a ladder onto the roof - it's more reliable, they won't get there right away.

The snow leopard did not come, the disappeared did not come, instead, completely different ones came. In the morning I wrote a statement to Khodzhent, to the district executive committee with the news of Baryshnikov's death and with a request to accept the meteorological station from me. My plan was very simple: go through the tugai to the main road and hand over a package to some person traveling to Khodzhent. Having addressed the package, I looked up and shuddered: in front of the open window stood and stared at me

---

[6] Tugai is a floodplain forest of river valleys in desert and semi-desert zones.

straight in the eye, a strange man, a Russian, about thirty years old, with a trimmed sandy moustache on a dry tanned face.

"Alone?" he inquired.

"One," I answered. "Where are you from?"

Behind the wall in the next room a floorboard creaked, someone was walking there. I got up to look.

"Sit still," said the man with the moustache. "Baryshnikov? How young…"

- I'm not Baryshnikov at all.

— Do you have any weapons?

- No.

— Raise your hands.

He climbed, or rather stepped, bending down, into the window, which was located very low, and ran his palms over my body from top to bottom.

- Go ahead.

I went out onto the porch and saw a second Russian there, broad-shouldered, stocky, with transparent blue eyes and gray hair at his temples. And to the side stood four saddled horses, supervised by two Uzbek policemen. I immediately realized that this elderly man was the boss of them all.

— Last name? — he asked. I gave my name.

- What are you doing here?

- Yes, I'm guarding a meteorological station.

- Where is Baryshnikov?

- Died.

There was silence. The Chekists exchanged glances. I had already realized that the Chekists had come to see me. The eldest, an elderly man, said:

- Really. And for a long time?

— The day before yesterday evening.

— Where did you bury him?

- I didn't bury them. Ivan Ivanovich Ivanov buried him. But I don't know - maybe he didn't bury him either.

- So you didn't take part in the funeral? I told him about my appearance here, about yesterday's trip to the village of Polvan-Tash to the mullah with a request to bury Baryshnikov according to the Muslim rite.

"But he was Russian, so why according to the Muslim rite?" asked the senior security officer.

— Before his death, he expressed a wish to be buried according to the ritual.

— Did you hear it yourself?

- No, I came here an hour after his death. Ivan Ivanovich told me.

- He's being sneaky! - the mustachioed Chekist grinned. - Come on, you're too young to be sneaky. We've had people like him crack.

"I have nothing to confess about," I replied.

"How many convictions?" asked the elder.

- Not a single one. I've never been on trial.

- How do you know the word "split"?

- I figured it out. It's not that hard.

— I don't advise you to be cunning.

And the old man handed me a booklet - an ID. "Korenev. Senior Inspector of the Central Investigation Department. Moscow," I read.

- So, you are from Moscow?

- Yes, from Petrovka. You remember, I bet?

- I can't remember, I've never been to Moscow.

After this, the security officers looked through Baryshnikov's reproductions, notebooks, and books. Korenev opened the package and read my statement to the Khodzhent District Executive Committee.

— Were you thinking of sending?

— That's why I wrote it.

The statement helped a lot. Korenev believed me. But he still sent me, accompanied by a policeman and a Chekist with a moustache, to Polvan-Tash so that the mullah could confirm his conversation with me yesterday. The mullah confirmed it, although he looked at me with a wolfish expression. The servants and the driver of yesterday's cart also confirmed it. My position was strengthened, and on the way back I was much more cheerful. And the Chekist with a moustache also moved away and now spoke to me willingly.

Korenev listened to his report and turned to me:

- I admit that you are telling the truth. I will check later, of course, but for now I admit it. But when you returned on the cart from Polvan-Tash and found no one here, did you suspect anything?

"I suspected," I replied.

- What exactly?

- Murder. Maybe it's very stupid...

"It's not stupid at all," Korenev interrupted me. "You suspected correctly. There is definitely murder here, if, incidentally, you are telling the truth."

— The pure truth.

- Then there is murder here. That is why they sent you to Polvan-Tash to the mullah, so that you would not interfere with hiding the body. Yes, you were lucky last night. Not this night, but the night before.

- What? - I didn't understand.

- Yes, because he's alive. It didn't matter to them whether they buried one or two.

True, they could have killed me! I was scared and felt my face turn pale. In general, I tend to get scared in retrospect, when the danger has already passed, the same thing happened to me during the war.

"And the body is hidden somewhere here, nearby," Korenev continued. "They couldn't have carried it far together."

"Maybe on some passing cart," I suggested.

- No, why would they show the dead man to another person? There's enough room around here. We'll look. You've helped us a lot, - he turned to me, already quite confidentially. - If we hadn't found anyone here, we'd have thought that Baryshnikov had simply left.

"And what business are you looking for him for?" I asked. Korenev remained silent in response.

And we started searching. We examined the shovels found in the neighboring house. Well, shovels are just shovels, you can't tell anything from them. Korenev, however, tried to dig the clay soil that had dried into stone. The shovels didn't take it. And on the other side of the houses, closer to the riparian zone, the soil was lower and much softer, and that's where we should start searching.

We searched all day, found nothing. In the evening one of the policemen went to Polvan-Tash, brought us flatbreads, sour milk and baked fish, crucified on willow forks. At dinner Korenev got angry and grumbled at me:

- You shouldn't have gone to the mullah at all. You should have gone away a bit, come back, sat down somewhere in the bushes and looked where they were burying.

- Yes, when I went to the mullah, I didn't suspect anything. That was later.

- Well, well! They are going to bury a Russian according to the Muslim rite, and he calmly goes to the mullah to negotiate, and no suspicions arise in his head! It's not even clear. After all, you saw these people for the first time! You should have suspected. Such a yawn! In the wanted list, you get kicked out of service for this.

And I was thinking of asking him about going to Moscow with him, about working as a wanted man. Now, of course, these are all pointless dreams.

The second day of searching did not bring any success either. Korenev became gloomy and only said:

- If there is a thread, there must be a knot. But where to look?

By "the knot" he meant Baryshnikov's corpse, by "the thread" - the matter for which he had come here from Moscow. Some very serious matter, probably political.

I went to sleep on the roof, but my eyes would not close, my thoughts would not become clouded. We were looking for Baryshnikov's grave in the tugai and near the tugai, but he could have been buried in the steppe, near the hills. Night birds were screaming, jackals were howling and laughing. Suddenly it dawned on me: why were the jackals howling not in the tugai, as last night, but in the open steppe? Perhaps they were attracted by the smell of decay, because they love cemeteries.

I went down the stairs. The policemen were sleeping near the horses, two of them on one felt mat. I woke them up, and at that moment Korenev's voice was heard from the open window:

- Who's there? What's going on?

It turned out that he was not sleeping either. Together we went towards the laughter and howling of the jackals, they flashed like grey shadows and ran away. The night was light, windless, after about fifteen steps I felt the stench of decay. Korenev felt it too and said in a trembling voice:

- Here!

At dawn the body was pulled out of a shallow depression filled with lumps of clay. I was sickened by the unbearable stench. The police kept their distance.

Korenev and his assistant examined the body and found no signs of violent death. But why then did they try to bury it secretly, without prying eyes? The matter was getting complicated.

"Go to Khodjent for the coffin," Korenev told his assistant. "We'll take it for an autopsy."

The windless, hot day dragged on for a long time. Two kites hung relentlessly over the sheet with which he had covered the dead man, sometimes, tilting, they described a slow circle in the sky and hung again. And they say that birds have no sense of smell. Korenev went into the room and sat there over Baryshnikov's notebooks. Then he called me.

- Could you describe the appearance of this Ivan Ivanovich? Give a verbal portrait.

I started to describe:

— Hair is tousled, half-gray...

- Well, let's say he'll comb his hair or take it off completely.

— He looks about forty years old... More like fifty.

- It's from a hangover. Was he really drunk?

- I think so.

- Or maybe not? No bottles of alcohol were found. Maybe he's not drunk, but drugged with some kind of drug?

— Does it make any difference?

— It does matter to us. Next. Eye color? Undefined. More precisely. Gray-green. Were his front teeth all intact? Didn't notice. Oh, you!

I continued to draw a verbal portrait, and it did not work out in words, but in my memory Ivan Ivanovich arose so clearly, as if he were sitting opposite me, and I heard his slightly hoarse voice, highlighting periods and commas in measured, rounded phrases, as if reading from a book. They say that everything in a person can change over the years, except for the voice, and Ivan Ivanovich's voice was familiar to me, once upon a time I had heard this voice somewhere... but where and when?

"Not much," said Korenev, looking through the written sheet. "But if you were to meet this Ivanov somewhere by pure chance, would you be able to recognize him?"

- Of course, I would have recognized it.

- So, if you meet... there is very little chance of this, but if you do, try to detain him.

— I would like some kind of paper from you to detain in case of a meeting.

- No, I can't give you such a piece of paper. But I can ask for it, since you are now involved in this matter anyway. That's why I'm asking.

He told me the gist of the matter in a few words. Several paintings by old masters - Rembrandt, Titian, Correggio - had been stolen from the Museum of Fine Arts in Moscow. This theft had stirred up the whole world. The total cost of the stolen paintings was estimated at two million, although in reality the paintings were simply priceless. In Moscow, persistent searches led to Ostankino, to the house of an old artist who was secretly painting a religious picture, while his son, a thirty-year-old blockhead, was studying the art of bell ringing. Both of them turned out to be not directly involved in this theft, but their trail led to Central Asia. No one would have bought the stolen paintings in the USSR, they were stolen "for export", and Central Asia was the most convenient border to cross. It was possible to find out with almost complete certainty that the stolen paintings were kept by Baryshnikov. Baryshnikov himself, or Avdeyev by his real name, was a wealthy Moscow man before the revolution, a connoisseur and collector of old paintings; the artist from Ostankino had once visited him. Having become entangled in one of the many conspiracies against the Soviet government, Avdeyev had fled Moscow back in 1921 and, under the name of Baryshnikov, had taken refuge in Central Asia, at a meteorological station. Here, in the deserted foothills, it was almost impossible to find him, but Korenev found him and came to him with his assistant. Only he was too late - Ivanov had appeared here earlier. The one-eyed old man was, by all indications, in cahoots with Ivanov, probably a former Basmachi, sent from the other side by the British, a guide across the border. If so, then the British were also involved in the theft of the paintings. However, all of this still needed to be verified, as did Ivanov's relationship with Baryshnikov: were they from the same criminal gang or from different, warring ones, or perhaps Ivanov acted completely independently, on orders received from that side?

"I'm not saying this for publicity," Korenev finished. "I'm only saying it because maybe you'll meet this Ivanov somewhere. So you'll know who you're detaining. And not alone, call someone for help."

I had, of course, read Conan Doyle and the cheap books in colorful covers - Nat Pinkerton, Nick Carter, the Russian detective Ivan Putilin. But to hear the story of a real major crime from a real detective, to talk to him alone, to be given the task of detaining the criminal if I happened to meet him! My head was spinning.

The Chekist with the moustache returned. Behind him, a cart dragged along lazily, its wheels crunching on the salt marsh, carrying a coffin.

"Your replacement will come tomorrow," the security officer told me. "They asked me to stay on duty one more night."

An hour later everyone left, took away the deceased, the reproductions, the books, the notebooks. And I spent another night on the roof, all alone between the river and the mountains. I couldn't sleep, the night was floating, filled with its sounds, jackals were howling and laughing in the tugai. And I thought persistently about Ivan Ivanovich - if only he would come, and I would be able to jump on him from the roof, throw him to the ground and tie him up! It is true that boyishness does not end with boyhood, but, gradually waning, accompanies a person for a long time, sometimes to the grave.

In the morning a new meteorological observer arrived from Khodzhent, nondescript, thin, wearing glasses, a canvas sweatshirt and sagging trousers. I handed over the point to him and with the same cart went to the railway.

"Stop, stop!" the new metnab shouted, running out onto the porch. "You forgot your notebook!"

I thanked him and took the notebook; and I still have it - Baryshnikov's philosophical notes on the Sistine Madonna. The cart passed the tugai, came out into the flat, dirty-whitish salt marsh steppe and floated, shaky and creaking, along the beaten road to the ferry. The sun was already scorching, the sky had turned grey and cloudy, the outlines of the hills had blurred and become indistinct, but the snow-capped peaks of the ridge, as always, shone with pristine whiteness. The cart driver stretched his right leg along the shaft and began an endless song about what he had seen on the way, and he saw the same thing: the dull greyish shine of the salt marsh, dry tufts of brown camel thorn, crested sand-coloured larks, falling vertically to the ground like stones. I closed my eyes and forgot myself, tired by the loose swaying of the cart.

I came to from a shout and a knock: we were on the bank of the Syr Darya, at the pier, and one of the carts that had arrived earlier was being loaded onto the ferry. The horse backed up, the driver lashed it in the belly, and finally the horse jumped convulsively through the crack separating the ferry from the pier, thundered its hooves on the boards, and the cart's huge wheels slowly rolled onto the plank flooring. A second cart approached for loading, and my driver moved a little to the side to water the horse; it, knee-deep in mud, slowly and for a long time sucked in the yellow water, swelling its sides, and the driver whistled thinly and quietly to it. Finally, we loaded up, and the ferrymen cast off, laboriously turning the seething steering oar. The water sparkled with a hot, blinding shine. And on the other bank the salt marsh steppe stretched out again, soon replaced by dunes covered with yantak.

It was here, in the dunes, that I caught myself: I was dozing and swinging on the cart, but I was persistently, with some occipital part of my brain, thinking about one thing: where and when had I heard Ivan Ivanovich's voice before?

Ahead of me I could already see the white, deserted, boring and bare building of the railway station; I had to go from here to Tashkent. There were still two hours left before the train, I let the driver go and went to look for a place in the shade. In the garden behind the station there were only small-leaved acacias with already yellowed pods, the shade here was transparent, as if from a stretched fishing net, and I wandered further in the sun, to the yellow tower of the water pumping station, and sat right on the ground, on the shady side. The concrete base of the tower was covered with inscriptions made in pencil, charcoal and chalk. "On February 12, Girka the Devil left for Bukhara", "From Murghab to Jalal-Abad, Guilty Pavel", "Stepan Prygunok, on tour in Kokand, passing through Khujand" and many other inscriptions. I knew before that railway water pumps are chosen by thieves, pickpockets and just vagabonds to inform each other about crossings. "Girka the Devil" and "Prygunok" are, of course, petty thieves, pickpockets, but "Vinovaty Pavel" is probably one of the big ones, maybe a safecracker, it is not for nothing that his handwriting is confident, large... I wonder if the criminal investigation department knows about the secret of railway water pumps? They probably don't know, but they could extract a lot of useful information for themselves from these inscriptions... But Ivan

Ivanovich will not write here, he is too big a bird... But where did I hear his hoarse voice? Where and when?..

This persistent inability to remember was already becoming painful, pushing aside all other thoughts. For the hundredth time I began to go over various incidents and encounters in my memory. No, it was all wrong. And suddenly my breathing stopped. Well, of course, here it is! Katya Smolina, the trial, Dr. Sidorkin's testimony... That's where I heard that voice! Dr. Sidorkin!.. How come I didn't recognize him right away!

Now I had to hurry to Khodzhent - perhaps Korenev was still there. I ran to the station. The Khodzhent cabbies were already arriving at the train in their shiny new phaetons, harnessed in pairs. Nowhere had I met such chic cabbies as in Kanibadam and Khodzhent - for two rubles they drove passengers dashingly, racing each other, hanging on the box, whooping, whistling and cracking a whip. This time my cabbie, hoping to turn around and still make it to the train, surpassed all records, whisked me to Khodzhent in a flash, grabbed the two rubles and raced back, hanging on the box, whooping, whistling and swinging a whip over his head.

I came to the district police station and asked about Korenev. "Here," the officer on duty answered. "Who's asking for him?" A minute later Korenev came out and he could tell from my face that I had brought important news. "This Ivan Ivanovich is actually..." I began, without even saying hello. "Wait," Korenev stopped me, "let's go." We went into an empty room next door.

- Well, what? - asked Korenev.

- This Ivan Ivanovich... I remembered... in fact, he is Doctor Sidorkin from the Kokand railway hospital.

- A doctor from Kokand! - Korenev stood up and closed the window. - You're great, that explains a lot.

"What exactly does it explain?" I asked, feeling I had the right to ask this question.

— The autopsy showed that Baryshnikov was poisoned with potassium cyanide.

I told Korenev about Katya Smolina, about Sidorkin, about Katya's trial.

- Now be quiet, don't tell anyone, - said Korenev. - That means he was in the service of the Basmachi for a long time. He could have entered the service of the English. What time does the train to Kokand leave?

- Now only in the evening, at half past nine.

- Take a walk for now, and come back in two hours - maybe we'll need some clarification.

Two hours is a long time if you have nothing to do. The market in Khodjent was small and besides, it was getting late; only the taverns and teahouses were doing business. So I wandered from tavern to teahouse and back to tavern again. On the other side of the river rose dark rocky cliffs, wild and bare; having heated up during the day, now, before evening, they breathed a dry and viscous heat on the city like an oven. I would have liked to swim... but the river in its steep, precipitous banks was so turbulent, yellow, in rapids and swirling funnels! I returned to the market square again. What can I say, I was a little offended by the calm with which Korenev listened to me. Such an important message! From whom else could he have received it? After all, now, if they catch Sidorkin and find the paintings, it will be my merit most of all, and meanwhile my name will remain unknown and Korenev will take all the honors. So I thought, without really putting any effort into this matter, taking credit for a purely accidental confluence of circumstances and overflowing with self-important touchiness - a very petty and nasty feeling, unfortunately characteristic of the young, and even more often the young than the old. This is, apparently, a distorted image of the constant striving of youth for self-affirmation, for the realization of its inner powers outwardly, with the obligatory thirst for universal recognition and admiration, that is, with insatiable ambition, or rather - vanity.

And I was immediately punished for my thoughts. I was just coming out of the alley onto the market square, I came out and backed away in bewilderment, in fear. On the opposite side of the square, on the platform of a poor, sooty teahouse, sat Ivan Ivanovich! I pressed myself against the fence, hid behind the trunk of a mulberry tree. Did he notice me or not? No, he didn't. Detain him? But I'm alone, and he could be armed. And even, probably, armed. Run to the police? But by that time he'll disappear... Then I saw the teahouse owner hand him a teapot. Aha, that means he's just come to the teahouse, he'll sit there for half an hour, I'll have time. And I rushed through the alleys, around the corner, to the police.

- Korenev! Quickly! - I shouted, bursting into the duty officer's room. They called Korenev, and the two of us rushed to the market, to the same alley from which I had seen Ivan Ivanovich.

We were not late, he was sitting in the teahouse.

"Wait here," said Korenev and went to him. I saw him approach him, sit down on the platform, start talking, and two minutes later call me with his hand. The closer I came, the harder it was for me to walk: I could already clearly see that the man in the teahouse was not Ivan Ivanovich at all – he was much younger and had a different face. I sat down next to Korenev and whispered to him:

- No... I was wrong.

The imaginary Ivan Ivanovich finished his tea and left, then Korenev, smiling, said:

- How could you have made a mistake, brother? But it is a bright day. Perhaps you are short-sighted?

"A little," I lied. "A little myopia."

- Then you need glasses, otherwise it will go from easy to hard. - Korenev stood up. - Well, I'm off to finish the report. And as for your thoughts about going with me to Moscow, to work in the criminal investigation department, I'll tell you straight - it's not worth it. Our work is unpleasant, terrible work. And you can't get any glory, because it's a dull job. Sometimes our people die, and in complete obscurity. I wish it would end soon, our work, completely, clean! Under communism there will be no such thing - that's good! And you need to take up your studies with both hands, that's the real thing for you. Well, good health!

He left. He didn't even invite me to see him off to the station. Total disdain! And what the hell do I need his advice for - to study, to grab hold of things with both hands! And then I realized that I had never once mentioned to him, not even a single word, about going to Moscow, about working in the criminal investigation department. I thought about it, but I didn't say it. How did he know my secret thoughts?

Now, when I often learn the secret thoughts of others, I am not surprised by Korenev, but then, I remember, I was immensely surprised, to the point of trembling. But I could no longer ask him, we never met again. Sidorkin's fate also remained unknown to me – was he caught or not. And the stolen paintings were found in Moscow, in Vsekhsvyatskoye: they were found buried in the ground under the floor of one of the little houses. The newspapers reported this in the early thirties, when I was already living in Moscow and studying. The paintings turned out to be badly damaged, but the newspapers expressed hope that they would be restored. I read the newspaper on the tram, on the way to the institute, and was very happy: it means that they had not managed to smuggle the paintings abroad, they had not managed after all! At the institute, I could not resist and told my fellow students about Korenev, about Baryshnikov, about Sidorkin, about the one-eyed old man and about myself, of course; I spoke with enthusiasm and suddenly faded, feeling that they did not believe me. It is generally difficult to talk about yourself: more often than not, they do not believe. Student Moshkov, small, with yellow chicken hair and angry, like all small ones, said in a creaky tenor:

- You will become a screenwriter, you definitely will, you write great.

Now I'm telling this story again. Maybe now you'll believe me?

I grew up, matured, and, as always happens, I didn't notice my maturation or the maturation of my peers.

And the new, Soviet world was, in essence, my contemporary. Great changes were taking place around me and before my eyes, I saw these changes and was not surprised by them. As if in the life of the ancient East it had always been so that the lands of landowners and mosques were distributed among the poor, that women uncovered their faces, that more and more new-method Soviet schools, technical schools, institutes, red teahouses and hospitals appeared.

I am writing about the first post-revolutionary decade in Central Asia. The required number of generations had not yet changed, and the new life was forging its way through with a fight. "Europeanization" was the most popular, the most ardent word among the youth. "Islam," the elders responded. And, as with every historical turn, the argument now and then turned into bloody clashes.

I happened to take part in one of these fights. By chance, everything went off without blood... but it could have, and it very well could have, it was very close!

Sometimes the question would occur to me: why did I get into various adventures so often in my youth? Was it because I had an excessive inclination for them? I was not such an adventurer, and besides, my adventures were always completely selfless. The point, apparently, is something else: the whole life of those years now seems to me like a huge, unheard-of adventure on a global scale, in order to get into a personal adventure, there was no need to look for it - no need to avoid, no need to hide, nothing more was required - the adventure itself found its heroes.

...Senior Inspector of the Central Investigation Department Korenev left to follow the killer to Kokand, and I stayed in Khodzhent, hoping that Korenev might still need me. Every morning I went to the post office and inquired about a telegram on demand. There was no telegram, two weeks passed, I realized that Korenev would not call me, and I began to think about my future fate.

My money was melting away, and there was no prospect of earning money in Khujand. The sign business here had been taken over by two dodgers, who greeted me rather sullenly when I came to them with an offer to join the business as a third partner. The main trump cards these dodgers had were images of exhibition gold medals and the inscription: "The company has existed since 1862." The only thing missing was a proud reminder: "Supplier to the court of His Imperial Majesty." Thanks to the efforts of these two dodgers, the entire trading Khujand turned out to be medaled, every teahouse had existed since 1862. And they charged a lot for their medals - twenty rubles for a sign! And I, a fool, took seven and a half - I didn't guess about the medals and 1862, it's my own fault.

The Kanibadam love drama still tormented my heart, but distantly and dully, as if many years later. One day at the bazaar I met an acquaintance from Kanibadam and learned from him that Tanya had gone somewhere. It would have been possible to return to Kanibadam and resume the sign trade, this time with medals, but after thinking it over, I decided not to return: the places were too memorable, and the disgusting Ishanbaev was sitting in his old place in the district executive committee. Where to now? And again my thoughts turned to the distant city of Ura-Tyube.

And again I didn't get to this city - I got sick. In the morning I woke up with a feeling of a viscous ache all over my body, and an hour later I was lying under two blankets, jumping up and down and chattering my teeth in a severe chill. This is how tropical malaria begins. The chills gave way to fever, the fever - to sweat and weakness. The next day everything repeated itself in the same order. Among the many mosquitoes that bit me in Khujand, there was one with malaria.

In those years, there was a shortage of doctors in Central Asia, and the Khujand outpatient clinic was run by a former military paramedic, a drunkard and a bribe-taker. For ten rubles, he prescribed me quinine injections every other day. Those were real injections, not like today's! It was dark before my eyes when the old blunt needle, like a rusty awl, with a strained squeak pierced my skin and climbed into my back. A blister swelled, then turned into a wooden numbness.

In two weeks half my back was dead, and the malaria had not weakened at all - the paramedic's quinine solution must have been old and stale. And I would have perished from malaria - many perished from it then - but the owner of the teahouse where I lived came to the rescue. He took me to a Chinese doctor in one of the remote quarters.

The Chinese, already an old man with a black braid down to his waist, treated me in a strange way. In the yard there was a round oven for making cakes in the form of a huge clay pot, fixed horizontally and washed by hot air from the firebox below. I would strip down to my panties and climb into this heated pot on rice straw, leaving only my head outside. The Chinese would keep me in the pot, in the unbearable heat, for about half an hour, then pour a cup of black herbal brew into my mouth, so disgusting that after drinking it, I would immediately vomit it all up. The healing session would end; on flimsy, soft legs, as if my bones had melted in the pot from the heat, I would go under the awning to lie down on a reed mat.

A barbaric, witch doctor treatment, you will say. Yes, it may be witch doctor, but after four days my malaria had noticeably subsided, attacks began to visit me every other day, and not daily, as before, and after another two weeks they stopped altogether - I recovered.

Since then I believe in Chinese medicine, especially when it comes to Asian diseases. And how can I not believe, if medicine is still neither a science nor an art, based entirely on experience and has no theory, and the Chinese, of course, have more experience with Asian diseases. One thing must be said - the way the old Chinese treated me, putting me in a clay pot, is not applicable to elderly people: the heart will not withstand it.

The Chinese man treated not only malaria. Among his patients was Yusup Mamedaliev, an Uzbek guy three years older than me. I don't remember what he was sick with, but it doesn't matter; the Chinese man also cured him in about three weeks. Yusup and I met at the Chinese man's and very soon, as only happens in youth, we became friends.

He was an orphan, a native of Khujand, had been teaching in Margilan for the last two years, and had quit that spring and returned to Khujand. Short, slender, with a hooked nose and dark, hot eyes, he was undoubtedly handsome, but he was very unsmiling. As it turned out later, he had serious reasons for this gloom; I guessed that his soul was crushed by a heavy stone, but I did not yet know what kind. And he was not inclined to emotional outpourings in the Russian manner - with his soul wide open. Uzbeks in general, as I have noticed, are very reserved, even secretive, and do not like confessions.

But sometimes Yusup would explode, and then he would turn especially pale and his eyes would bulge like an enraged leopard. I deliberately avoid the comparison with a cat's eyes, it's too petty, leopard is the right word.

Yusup knew Russian very well, because he was brought up in an orphanage, among Russian boys. He read a lot, his favorite poets were Pushkin and Mayakovsky. In Pushkin, however, he was embarrassed by his noble origins and closeness to the royal court, he adored Pushkin somehow bashfully. But he loved Mayakovsky with proud frankness. Already at our second meeting, he read me his translation of "The Left March" into Uzbek. It was not just a good translation, it was an inspired translation. Yusup read in a low voice, slightly pale, and the refrain of the march "Chopkul, chopkul, chopkul" sounded in Uzbek with the same striking force as in Russian: "Left, left, left!"

But he rejected the great poets of the East outright – Firdausi, Hafiz, Saadi, Khayyam and Navoi. In this way, perhaps with a heavy heart, he paid tribute to his extreme rigorism. "We need Europeanization, but where are these poets calling us?" he said. "They are calling us back to Islam, to Sufism[7]. No, we have suffered enough from all this old stuff, we are three hundred years behind, we must catch up with Europe by car, and all these poets are camels. There is no place for them in the new life, the times of camel caravans are over!"

I remember our argument about the Uzbek theatre. I suggested an open stage, and in front of it a large platform, a sort of large teahouse, where the audience would sit on the floor and drink tea during the performance. Yusup turned pale, his lips trembled.

"A colonizer!" he said. "You are a real colonizer!"

I was offended and angry.

- Why a colonizer? On the contrary, I show respect for national customs.

- National customs! - he shouted in a high voice. - Mosques, dervishes - these are your national customs! Robes, ichigi, leather galoshes! Covered women! And you want to preserve all this! Why? To make it easier to rule over us!

In general, we often quarreled, which shows that our friendship was sincere. Almost always, I gave in and was the first to make peace. I gave in this time too, and we agreed that the Uzbek theater should be built according to the pan-European model: with a cloakroom, a buffet, a stalls, and a dress circle, but without boxes - in Yusup's

---

[7] *Sufism* is a teaching that is widespread in the Muslim world about the ways to achieve the highest grace, about knowing God, approaching Him and uniting with Him.

opinion, boxes were an expression of an outdated anti-democratic spirit.

But how infinitely sweet and tactful Yusup became after each quarrel, as if he was apologizing to me for his victory. He was a good guy, a very good guy, and I am glad that I had the chance to help him in a big and important matter. But more on that later.

I lived in the bazaar, in a teahouse, and Yusup rented a room from a farmer. His relationship with the owner, a former poor man, a chayriker, that is, a sharecropper, was curious. He worked for many years for one-third of the harvest on waqf land, that is, on land belonging to the mosque. Usually, chayrikers gave half of the harvest to their landlords, but there were losers who got waqf lands - then they had to give two-thirds. For the sanctity of the allotment, as I think.

After the revolution, during the land reform, the waqf lands were taken away from the mosques and distributed among the peasants. Yusup's owner received his plot in full and undivided ownership, and now he did not have to give the mullah anything. But it is not for nothing that the word "Islam" in Arabic means "submission", and the word "mussulim" means "submissive". The mullah's income from the waqf plot, of course, decreased, but did not dry up completely: every Friday in the mosque after prayers, he collected two or three rubles in voluntary donations from his former sharecroppers. It was these exactions that Yusup could not reconcile himself to and tirelessly shamed his owner. The latter listened to Yusup with respect, but did not refuse the mullah, foreseeing the afterlife and his answer before Allah.

Yusup tried to explain to him that there was no afterlife. The owner disarmed Yusup with a question:
- Where will my soul go after death?
- And there is no soul!
- Why do I dream at night? The cat sleeps and doesn't dream, but I do.

"How do you know that the cat doesn't dream, did she tell you?" Yusup shouted back.

Here the owner began to laugh.

— Just think: a cat sees dreams, ha-ha-ha!.. He was generally a cheerful, laughing person, this master, long years of backbreaking labor and poverty did not harden, did not dry up his life-loving soul.

"Aha!" he would exclaim, having read these lines, "you wrote "soul", so it exists, you wrote it yourself!" That was approximately the level at which he and Yusup had their weekly theological debates on Fridays. Now he has long since died, this master, and from his own experience he was convinced that he did not carry an immortal soul in his body during life. Frankly speaking, for his love of life, kindness and cheerfulness, I would gladly supply him with such a desired soul for his long journey, if it were in my power.

One day Yusup invited me to his place for pilaf. We sat in the garden, in the shade of an elm tree, Yusup put two bowls and a bottle of port wine on the tablecloth.

"Do you drink wine?" I asked in surprise.

"Is it European law to sit down to the table without wine?" he replied.

The port was bad, home-made. Yusup drank a whole glass, his face wrinkled, he drank with disgust. I realized that he was drinking on purpose, with the special purpose of violating the religious prohibition.

We finished the pilaf and moved on to tea.

"Are you a member of the Komsomol?" I asked.

"Why are you asking?" he answered a question with a question.

— Judging by your views, you should be a member of the Komsomol.

— I am a member of the shower, but I don't have a ticket.

- But why?

He paused, then said reluctantly:

— Origin gets in the way.

- But you grew up in an orphanage!

- But my father was a muezzin, a servant of the mosque. He was not a mullah, of course, but still from the clergy.

"Listen," I said, "nobody is forcing you to speak. You were left an orphan, and you might not even know anything about your father."

- I would be glad not to know anything about him, but I do. Anyone who joins the Komsomol must tell the whole truth about themselves. And if I tell them, they might not accept me.

- Maybe they will accept it.

- And if not, then what? And he turned pale.

"It's nothing," I said thoughtlessly. "Everything will remain as it is now."

"No," he said. "As it is now, it won't remain. Then I must go over to the enemies of the Soviet power. And I cannot go over to the enemies of the Soviet power, because it raised me, because it is a just power. What should I do then? Die?.."

I did not expect such an extreme conclusion and in my heart I regretted that I had started this conversation. Yusup noticed my confusion and consoled me:

- I will join the party straight away. When you are accepted into the Komsomol, they trust a person in advance, based on his origin. Because what deeds can you ask of a boy? But they accept you into the party differently, they judge a person by his deeds. First, I will accomplish some great Soviet deed, and only then will I apply to the party. I will accomplish such a deed that my origins will be forgotten. Soon I will leave Khodzhent in search of such a deed.

It was already getting dark, the mosquitoes began to buzz. Then a fresh wind blew from the river, the mosquitoes disappeared, the moon rose, and we all sat and talked, choosing a worthy deed for Yusup, after which he could certainly count on being accepted into the party. I advised him to volunteer for the Red Army while it was not too late, while the remnants of the Basmachi gangs were still roaming the mountains. He agreed with me, the only problem was that he did not know how to shoot a rifle. "It's nothing, you'll learn in two weeks, it's very simple!" I exclaimed with such an air as if I myself were a famous marksman. "Perhaps you're right," Yusup responded thoughtfully. "I don't have a family and never will. The Red Army is a suitable place for me. Now I know that I will remain single forever."

We finished our port wine, Yusup became talkative, losing his usual dry restraint, and told me the story of his life and his unsuccessful love.

The muezzin's asset is his voice. It must be strong but soft, thick but not hoarse, and by the end of the chant it must gradually rise, turning into the finest thread; the whole secret is that this thread should stretch infinitely long and, gradually dying away, remain clearly audible over a long distance. "In the morning, the muezzin, on the finest thread of his voice, pulls the sun from beyond the edge of the earth; at midday, the muezzin's voice is thick and coppery, like a trumpet; in the evening, on the silver thread of his voice, he lowers the sun beyond the edge of the earth..."

I remember the evening voices of the muezzins over the expanses of fields and gardens, covered in a light fog; these silver threads, trembling, stretched from all sides, filling the soul with sadness and sweetness. Now, when they have fallen silent almost everywhere, replaced by the voices of radio megaphones, I do not regret them: everything has its time. But still, in any antiquity, even the most difficult and dark, there was its own beauty.

Muezzins, like Russian deacons, were a special class in the Muslim clergy. Severe Islam, born at the dawn of global Arab power from the roar of battle trumpets and the continuous rumble of battle drums, was completely devoid of any signs of lush rituals - a stingy, extremely simplified religion of warriors. But any religion must have its own beauty and its own artists. In fulfillment of this rule, Catholicism brought organists to churches, Orthodoxy - deacons with disproportionately powerful basses, and Islam - muezzins.

The same chant five times a day! The artistic possibilities of the muezzins were cruel. Someone said: the stricter the restrictions facing a true artist, the more they serve to perfect his craft. It is difficult to imagine restrictions stricter than those that Islam placed on artists: for example, Islam forbade painters from depicting living beings, and the artist with all his talent went into ornament. And indeed, in ornament, some achieved unheard-of mastery. But where there are restrictions, there are overseers: true painting was not born from ornament, just as true vocal art was not born from the singing of the muezzins.

Yusup's father - I am basing this on Yusup's own story - was a great artist at heart. Once, not long before the revolution, the main mosque in Shakhrisabz announced a muezzin competition. Twelve competitors gathered, each was given a full day, five chants. And all twelve days during the hours of the azan, that is, the call to prayer, the square in front of the mosque was filled with Shakhrisabz residents, connoisseurs of singing. The most sophisticated connoisseurs began listening near the minaret, then went further and further, and in the end listened from the outskirts of the city, where the chants could barely be heard.

Yusup's father prepared for the competition long and thoughtfully. To his talent and skill he added thought. He sang all five calls to prayer to the same tune, but in different ways: in the morning call there was joy and gratitude for the new day sent to the world, at midday the singer's voice sounded coppery and thick, reminding of the day's labors, after sunset - with peaceful sadness towards the night. All the Shakhrisabz connoisseurs were completely delighted and unanimously predicted victory for such a special singer. He himself believed in his victory and until the end of the competition - he sang on the fifth day - he was in a happy half-sleep. He was invited to visit from house to house one after another and rewarded with gifts. The thirteenth day arrived - the day of judgment. Among the judges were two akhunds from Bukhara, two withered old men with long gray beards, casting a dull yellow tint, with eyes burning with a dull and gloomy flame. They both said in agreement:

- This muezzin should not even be allowed on the minaret. He was supposed to sing about God, about the heavenly, but he sang about the earthly: about the sun, about midday and earthly labors, about evening and going to bed. This is blasphemous! And it would be necessary to check how firm he is in Islam and how diligent he is in fulfilling the Sharia.

Here they are, the guards! Yusup's father, of course, did not receive any distinction for his singing. The rumor of his apostasy blew away all his admirers like the wind, he was left alone with his grief, with his insult. He could not stay in Shah-Rizabs, and he took his son and went far away, to Khujand. He made the right choice: Khujand was far from Bukhara, and the power of the dead Islamist dogma was not so felt here.

But in Khujand a new misfortune awaited him: he began to lose his voice. From the main mosque he had to move to a smaller one, and then to an even smaller one, on the outskirts.

Soon he died, Yusup left Khujand and became a street child. Before leaving, he had a serious conversation with twelve-year-old Kutbia, the daughter of a soap maker, they agreed to get married when they grew up. And so six years passed, they grew up, and Yusup came to Khujand to ask Kutbia if she remembered her promise? She was already under the veil and told him that she remembered, but could not fulfill it, because her father had arranged for her to marry a rich cattle merchant. Yusup asked if she wanted to go to the merchant's house as a third wife. She began to cry. Yusup repeated his question and in response heard that it would be easier for her to die, but everything had already been decided and nothing could be done.

Yusup did talk to her father; the conversation was short: yes, Qutbiya was betrothed and a ransom was received for her. Now Yusup was going to leave Khujand for the second time, and forever.

"So you love her if you came back after six years," I said. "That's why you decided to remain a bachelor for the rest of your life."

He remained silent; after all, there still lived in him a fatalistic resignation to fate - the blood of his ancestors.

- And you agree to give her away so easily, Yusup!..

— If I could give a bigger ransom...

- What does ransom have to do with it? To hell with it, this ransom! No, Yusup, I see that in reality you are not a fighter for a new life, in reality you are a defender of the old.

It was impossible to hurt him more. He flared up.

- What can be done? Tell me if you know!

- And I will tell you!

- Well, speak up.

- I'll think about it and then I'll tell you.

- Big deal... I've been thinking about it for a whole month and haven't come up with anything.

We parted after a quarrel. It is, of course, not very polite for a guest to quarrel with his host, but the subject of our conversation was too serious: human destiny - or rather, two destinies.

The next day, passing by the city garden, I saw a poster promising a variety of cheerful divertissement in the evening, including a theatrical and satirical reading of A. S. Pushkin's poem "Count Nulin". I took two tickets and suddenly remembered that Yusup and I had quarreled. If I brought him a ticket, he would think that I was, as always, giving in, looking for reconciliation, and this time I did not want to give in. In the evening I went to the show alone. It was boring - a decrepit magician showed simple tricks, constantly persuading the audience that there were no miracles in his tricks, but only sleight of hand, but the audience did not see any special sleight of hand, and did not even think about miracles. Then a juggler in dirty tights twirled and tossed four large wooden bottles, then two fat women in sailor suits performed the "Matchish" dance with stony faces, and then came the turn of the theatrical-satirical reading.

The performers - there were two of them - brought a long table with many different objects on it onto the stage. Then the first performer - the reader - stood to the right of the table, and the satirical

94

theatricalist - to the left. The reader was young and lively, with a wavy hairdo of a hot curl and a black mustache in an arrow, and the theatricalist, a man of about forty, was corpulent, muzzled and sullenly looked at his feet.

"Count Nulin," a poem by Alexander Pushkin, the reader announced in a circus voice, playing with his dark eyes, and began:

It's time, it's time! The horns are blowing...

The big-faced theatrical performer took a tin horn from the table and, puffing out his cheeks, blew into it.

The hounds in hunting gear are already sitting on their horses at dawn…

The big-faced man put a cardboard tricorne with a tassel on his head and, spreading his legs, began to jump up and down in one place, as if in a saddle.

Greyhounds jumping on leashes...

Here the big-faced theatrical performer bent over at a right angle, lowered his arms as if getting down on all fours, and barked in a thin voice at the audience: "Woof, woof, woof!.."

Then this disgrace continued in the same vein, the line being especially colorfully illustrated:

There's a flask of rum in my bosom...

Mordaty pulled an aluminum flask from his bosom and sucked on it, then, wincing and spitting, he bit into a pickled cucumber. He did it very naturally, and the audience groaned enviously.

Yes, my youthful encounters with the world of theatrical art did not help to cultivate in me love and respect for this world. To this day I am afraid of the theater and very rarely go to performances. Cinema, circus are another matter, but the theater is not for me. As soon as the curtain opens on any, even the best theater, I immediately remember the theatrical-satirical reading, and everything is lost. That is the power that certain memories have over us!

It was unbearable to listen to Count Nulin any longer, so I stood up and went to the exit.

In the middle rows I saw Yusup. We met eyes, he stood up and followed me out.

"Well, how did you like the reading?" I asked.

"It's a disgrace, a disgrace!" he replied in an angry voice. "Where are they looking up there, why are they allowing this?"

The teahouses had not yet closed. We went to a small teahouse on the banks of the Syr Darya. The platform of the teahouse was fixed on poles, leaning obliquely against the bank, and hung over the water itself, which angrily seethed and grumbled beneath us.

"But he did drink real moonshine from a flask," I said, continuing the conversation about the theatrical reading. "There's nowhere to get rum, so moonshine will do. 'For want of a stamp, we'll write it on a simple one.'"

"What kind of drink is rum?" Yusup asked. "I've never seen it."

- I haven't seen it either, but I know it's made from sugar cane. The best rum is Jamaican, it's very famous all over the world.

- Very strong, I guess.

- Yes. A sailor's drink. Or rather, even a pirate's drink. Pirates loved it very much.

- And now they don't like it?

— They would love even now, only they are no more, the pirates.

— Were these people pirates?

- Pirates are sea robbers. They sailed the seas on their ships and robbed merchant ships.

We talked about rum, about pirates... We had to talk about something. Yusup suddenly fell silent, as if looking into himself, and confessed:

- Yesterday I was wrong, forgive me. Indeed, I submitted in my soul to the laws of antiquity, and I should not submit to them. You promised to think about it, have you thought about it?

To be honest, I didn't even remember his case that day due to lack of time, but I said fearlessly:

- Yes, I thought...

Or maybe I really was thinking about his case, but I didn't notice it. After all, there are such dark thoughts that for a long time and unknown to a person, they hide somewhere in the depths of the mind and soul before they surface and take a clear form in words.

"What do you say?" he asked. It dawned on me.

- Qutbiya must be stolen!

- What do you mean steal it? - Yusup was amazed.

"We live in the East, and in the East, girls have always been stolen since ancient times.

- It was once, but now it is not, thank God.

- So be it, if not! Why can't we turn the custom of the past to the benefit of the new, when it is necessary? Is it better to destroy both ourselves and Qutbiya?

"Quiet!" Yusup whispered. I really had gotten carried away and started speaking too loudly, and the teahouse owner, sitting by his samovar, was looking anxiously in our direction.

- Do you think this is possible?

I heard a renewed hope in Yusup's voice.

"Of course!" I exclaimed in a whisper and remembered a book I had read long ago.

— Why do escapes even from prison succeed? Because the prisoner thinks more about how to escape than the jailer thinks about how to guard the prisoner. But your Qutbia is not behind bars, and there is no guard near her! It's all about who will think more!

We sat in the teahouse until midnight, instilling anxiety in the teahouse owner's heart: they were shouting, whispering, they must be plotting something evil… He sighed with relief, receiving money from us. We parted. But I couldn't fall asleep – my restless head was in full swing, and by morning the plan was ready.

When I came to Yusup, it turned out that he had also come up with a plan overnight, and I was very surprised that our two plans agreed on almost everything, as if they had been thought up by one person. First, we had to persuade Qutbiya to escape. This part of the plan was the most troubling. What if she didn't agree – then everything would go to hell. But Yusup assured me that she would agree, that she would definitely agree. We had completely changed places: at first I was the leader, and he was the follower, and also a reluctant one (traces of Eastern fatalism), and now, having set off, he developed such speed and energy that I couldn't keep up with him. It was decided that in two days he would try to see Qutbiya and talk to her - on Friday, at the hour of prayer, when the trembling threads of the call would stretch from all the minarets of Khujand and the Muslims, submitting to him and shuffling their leather galoshes on the dry earth, would head to their mosques. Yusup, the muezzin's son, turned all the muezzins of Khujand into accomplices in our conspiracy. In general, I considered the choice of this day and hour wise: people in the mosques, fewer eyes.

The second difficulty of the plan was this: if Qutbiya agreed, how to kidnap her? At first we thought - at night, then we rejected this way. Summer nights are short and bright, Qutbiya can catch someone's eye. A girl on the street at night! There will inevitably be a ruckus. During the day it would be easier to take her out of the yard, but how then to get her to the station to the train? In Khujand there were eight cabbies on hand, women rode in cabbies very rarely and only when accompanied by their husbands, of course, the cabbie would be surprised by such strange passengers as Yusup and Qutbiya, he might even refuse to seat them and raise a fuss.

"On horseback!" I suggested.

Yusup clicked his tongue negatively - where to get horses? Besides, Kutbia hardly knows how to ride, because she is Uzbek, not Kyrgyz. The idea of escaping on horseback in the French manner in the style of Dumas had to be abandoned. And how nice it would be: two lovers, two horses, spread out, racing along the road, escaping from pursuit!..

On foot? But it's twelve miles to the station, three hours' walk in front of people. Maybe I should make a deal with the cabbie in advance? No, he'll sell out of greed or fear.

We became despondent - these twelve miles to the station turned out to be a big obstacle.

"If a man had to flee, it would be easier," Yusup said. "In the spring, here in Khojent, they tried one Basmachi, he hid for a whole year under women's clothing, under a black veil, and they couldn't catch him.

Why did he remember this Basmach? Apparently, he had already embarked on the path of guesswork, only from the other end.

Basmach, a man under women's clothing! Let's turn it around - let it be a woman, a girl in men's clothing!

- In European men's clothing! - Yusup picked up. - People from the region often come to us in Khodzhent, to the district committee of the Komsomol. Then they leave. The cabbies are used to it.

Thus was born our simple and fantastic plan; if it succeeded, it was only because it was boyishly fantastic.

The following Friday, at the hour of the afternoon prayer, we went to Qutbiyah's house. I remained on the corner, on guard, and Yusuf dove into the alley, to the fence enclosing the garden.

About ten minutes later he returned. His trousers were stained with grey clay at the knees. I realized: the fence was high, and he was pulling himself up on his hands to look in.

"She's not in the garden, she must be in the house," he said.

- Watch, Yusup, maybe she will come to the garden after all.

— They might notice me in the alley.

- Jump over the fence, hide in the garden somewhere in the bushes and wait.

He disappeared, I walked to the opposite side of the road, to the shade of old willows above a small pond. From here the alley was clearly visible, it was deserted. Then an old man on a grey donkey appeared in the distance, rode out onto the main road and turned towards the market, then two covered women came out of the alley and also turned towards the market, and I, watching them, tried to guess by their gait which was younger and which was older. I waited a long time, the sun was setting in golden dust, and on the ground in the shaded places the evening twilight was already thickening, the smell of mud wafted towards me from the pond. Yusup was still not there, had he been caught?.. Finally he appeared, waved his hand at me: let's go. He walked quickly along one side of the road, I walked level with him on the other, we did not come closer, did not even look at each other. "Why are we walking apart, as if leaving a corpse behind us," I thought. I crossed the road and approached Yusupov, he was pale.

"Well?" I asked.

"I almost got caught," he replied. "When we were talking, her uncle came into the garden. It's surprising that he didn't notice me in the bushes, I wasn't ten steps away."

- So you talked to her?

- Of course I did. She agreed.

- Have you set a day?

- Yes, the day after tomorrow, at the same time.

- The day after tomorrow! - I exclaimed. - Are you crazy! We don't have anything ready yet and we don't have a man's suit for her! Why did you make the appointment so quickly?

- It wasn't me, she appointed it herself. They want to send her to the mountains for the summer, her uncle came for her.

Frankly, I was surprised by Qutbia's character: she decided right away, in one minute. So much for the downtrodden, oppressed woman of the East! But she decided so quickly because the East itself had already changed and she could already decide for herself.

Yusup described Kutbia's figure to me: average height, very thin, which means the suit needs to be the smallest size, for a teenager.

Life in Khodjent began early because of the daytime heat, shops were already open at seven o'clock. The next morning I went to the Tsentrosoyuzovsky store. There were no ready-made clothes there, they could only offer me a men's straw hat and boots. The state-owned store had only one canvas suit - huge, made for a fat man. I had to take it with the expectation of alteration.

Near the bazaar lived a Russian tailor: "Accepting orders, as well as refacing and repairs." His sign was like all the others, decorated with a gold medal and the inscription "The company has existed since 1862." Yusup and I knocked on the gate. No one answered. We entered the courtyard and saw the tailor. Shaggy, in only underpants, barefoot, he was creeping along the sunlit wall and catching someone invisible on it. He would slap his palm, then, squeezing the emptiness with his fingers, he would examine it for a long time and carefully.

The tailor's wife appeared in the doorway and came up to us.

- What a change! - she said unfriendly, having listened to us. - Can't you see for yourself - he went into the lane.

Then I realized that the tailor had gone on a drinking binge and was now hunting devils on the wall.

"Come back in a week, he'll have come to his senses by then!" the woman said.

In a week! We couldn't afford to lose even one hour. I began to persuade the woman to take on the redo personally.

"We won't ask about the quality," I said. "Whatever it takes, that's fine, as long as it's done on time. Five rubles... Six... Well, seven if you want!"

She hesitated.

- Yes, here it is, an idol! He'll take your suit and drink it!

The tailor had indeed already noticed the bundle in my hands and was taking a look at it with a predatory, burning gaze, having forgotten about catching devils.

"Should I finish him off?" the woman said hesitantly. "Buy him another bottle, the damned thing, he'll be blind by tomorrow."

A bottle of moonshine was bought, the tailor was given a drink, locked in the henhouse, the woman got to work, and the next morning we received the altered suit. As I was counting out seven rubles for the woman, the door of the henhouse suddenly opened with a bang, and the tailor ran out into the yard, even more disheveled than yesterday, with chicken feathers and fluff in his hair.

- Stop! - he shouted, rushing towards us. - Stop! Who are you?

And suddenly he froze, seeing the money in his wife's hands. We went out into the street. From the yard we heard the woman's cries:

- Not yours, don't come near, unclean spirit, I won't give it up!..

"He'll beat her," Yusup said.

We returned, opened the gate and left, reassured. There really was a beating going on in the yard, only it wasn't the tailor who was beating his wife, but she was beating him. She was beating him with raw cow liver, very cleverly and deliciously, guessing by the cheeks, now to the right, now to the left, and at the same time loudly calling for help - a common female tactic.

Yusup and I spent the whole day together, not knowing what to do with ourselves or what to do. In the garden, the leaves were shimmering with sunbeams, the turtledove's wings were rustling, the hoopoes were sitting on the ground, raising their crests, and the oriole was crying out with a lonely, bright voice. The day was windy, cool, with high, thin clouds in the blue sky, with a cheerful play of shadows and sunspots on the grass. After midday, the wind died down. I looked at my watch. It was time to get down to business.

The hour of the pre-evening prayer and the hour of departure of the cabbies for the evening trains did not coincide. I went to the house of one cabbie and woke him up. Would he leave for the station in an hour? "In an hour? Why?" he asked.

"There are no trains at this time." "A very important person is leaving," I explained. "A carriage with a locomotive will be waiting for him at the station." "Who is this person?" the cabby was curious. "It's a secret," I said. "After his departure, there will be a big fuss in Khujand."

This should not have been said at all: after all, the cabby has relatives and acquaintances. However, he will not have time to blab in one hour. I promised him three rubles instead of two for the ride, and he was convinced that he was really an important person. "Harness up, be ready, we will be there in an hour." - "Hop, maily," the cabby answered, "I still have time to wash the carriage."

I left, and just above Khujand, from all the minarets, the voices of the muezzins were heard. Our time. Fifteen minutes later we were in the alley, by the fence. I offered my back to Yusup, he jumped into the garden. Rustling, crackling - he was hiding in the bushes. And I had nowhere to hide in the narrow alley. I went to the opposite side of the alley, diagonally, but so that I could hear the whistle, our signal, from here. A woman came out of a nearby gate, I walked towards her with a carefree look, let her pass me, waited and returned to my previous place. Qutbiya was probably already changing her clothes. Damn it, how long did it take her to change! I left my place two more times and walked towards random passers-by with a carefree look. But there was still no whistle. Another passerby appeared, and as I approached him, I went cold: it was Yusup's owner, the same one who didn't believe in cat dreams.

There are such inopportune meetings!

- A-a-a! - he shouted, seeing me. - Hello, what are you doing here? I was visiting my brother, in the village. My brother lives well, under the reform he was given six tapans[8] of land and exempted from taxes for three years. Just think - for three years!.. What do you think, if I file an application, they can also exempt me from taxes? Maybe I'll have to slip a couple of chervonets to someone in the district executive committee. That's okay, I'll slip it to them. Do you think Yusup will write me such an application?

He said all this standing still, not continuing his way, and the minutes flew by, and delay threatened disaster. I never wished premature death on anyone, and now I sincerely regretted that he was returning from his brother's on his own feet, and not on a funeral stretcher - with a soul or without a soul, it makes no difference, as long as it is on a stretcher!

- Yes, yes, Yusup will write, - I answered, randomly mixing up the words, as if in delirium. - He will definitely slip it... that is, he will write it. And he will have to slip it to the tax... that is, to the district executive committee... Well, goodbye, we need to hurry.

- Wait, wait! - he shouted after me. - I haven't finished yet... wait, I tell you!

I waved my hand and quickened my pace. I was going into the depths of the alley, and after about fifty steps I looked back. My interlocutor finally moved, walked, or rather dragged himself, barely able to move his legs. What if he met another acquaintance! Fortunately, he didn't. Two minutes later I was in my place, by the

---

[8] *Tapan* - apparently there is a memory error here and what is meant is tanab, an old measure of area that varies in different regions: from one sixth to half a hectare.

fence, and just in time. Yusup whistled. "Hurry up, while there's no one here!" I answered. Kutbia appeared over the fence, standing on Yusup's back. I caught her and lowered her onto the road. Then a bundle fell at my feet, Kutbia's dress – so that no one would guess that she was changing – and three seconds later Yusup himself climbed over the fence. I remember that fence, tall, grey, blank, merging with the blind walls of the houses – the old East didn't want to see anything outside, it looked only inside itself, and we had so brazenly intruded from the side! We quickly walked forward, to the main road, we walked in single file: me, the girl, Yusup, and I was afraid to look back and kept quickening my steps. On the road it became easier for us, and we walked in a row, Qutbia in the middle. Qutbia's hair was very well tucked under a straw hat, but his trousers were wide, they were slipping down - we had not thought to buy a trouser belt. I had to give mine away, now my trousers were starting to slip down, and I was holding them up by sticking my fingers in my pockets.

- Kutbia, hide your face when you get into the carriage. And don't say anything, your voice will give you away.

She was confused, pale, and, forgetting that she was dressed as a man, she trotted along like a woman. It seemed to me that everyone we met immediately, at first glance, penetrated our secret.

Here is the cabbie's house, we have finally arrived! The cabbie drove out of the gate, his carriage was shining and glittering. We sat down, Yusup and Kutbia on the seat, and I - opposite, on the folding bench, facing them. We drove off. The cabbie often looked back, apparently trying to guess who the important person was here, for whom he had washed his carriage. And I was tormented: how could I not have realized that Kutbia should have been seated on the folding bench, with her back to the cabbie, so that he would not see her face.

But he saw. And guessed. He didn't turn around again, and that's how we arrived at the station. Yusup and Kutbia went into the building, and I stayed by the carriage to pay. Having accepted three rubles from me, the cab driver asked:

— Where is the carriage with the locomotive?

"He hasn't arrived yet," I replied. "Wait for me, I'll go back. Here's a ruble as a deposit."

He took the ruble, a grin twitching his moustache. Of course, he realized that I was deliberately keeping him at the station, preventing him from returning to the city, where the alarm might already have been raised.

…The station's passenger hall, empty and echoing, was filled with the sleepy, languid buzzing of flies; Yusup and Kutbiya were sitting next to each other on a hard wooden sofa. The sofa was chained to the wall with a thick chain to prevent theft. Kutbiya took off her straw hat, her pigtails fell down, and at that moment the station attendant came out of the service room into the hall, a young man with freckles, wearing a red cap larger than his head and slipping down onto his protruding ears, just like the boys who wear their father's cap. He looked in amazement at the Uzbek woman in a man's suit, but said nothing and disappeared with an important air behind the ticket office door.

"Kutbia should not be kept in sight," Yusup said. "In an hour, people will start arriving at the train. She had better change into women's clothes."

But then it turned out that Kutbiya didn't have a chachvana in her bundle – a black net made of horsehair for her face. She came out to Yusup in the garden without a chachvana. And in a woman's dress with her face uncovered!.. No, it was impossible to change clothes, and it was also impossible to wait here in the hall. Where to? I led the fugitives across the tracks to the familiar water pumping station, and we sat down on the shady side. Many new inscriptions were added to the concrete base of the water pumping station, I remembered one: "Pasha Brilliantovy". "Too sophisticated a nickname for a pickpocket, too easy for a big thief in law, must be some kind of swindler," I thought on the surface of my mind, but deep down I continued to think about the same thing: how will we manage to complete our task? The danger had not yet passed, Yusup and Kutbiya were not yet on the train.

Beyond the water pump, the salt marsh steppe gleamed dully in the low light of the evening sun; along the railroad stretched a chain of camels, led by a donkey, on whose back sat a caravan driver, singing his song in a thin, throaty voice. It was very quiet; the caravan driver's voice, though faint, reached us. "Here I am, riding, riding, riding," sang the caravan driver. "Here are my camels, they are coming, coming, coming… I am riding, and my camels are coming after me… I am riding in front, and they are coming behind… I am riding, riding, riding…" A whitish, bare salt marsh, a whitish, empty sky above it, a whitish fog on the horizon, and not a single bird in the sky. A dull expanse—it made one's head spin languidly and sleepily, and no other song could be born here except the endless one that the caravan driver was singing. And here, next to this ancient empty chamber, with this drawn-out song, there are three of us: two guys and the girl we stole. Just think!..

The station bell rang sharply, announcing the departure of a passenger train from Melnikovo to Khodzhent. The ticket office will open now. I ran to the station, stood fourth in line and took two tickets.

In an hour it would all be over, Yusup and Kutbia would already be on their way. Having handed Yusup the tickets, I leaned against the base of the water tower and closed my eyes. This day had left me incredibly tired, as if I had not slept for three days in a row. The ground began to float gently beneath me. To dispel my drowsiness, I stood up and decided to take a walk, but having taken the first step beyond the water tower, I immediately jumped back. On the platform I saw our cabby and with him an unfamiliar man in a silk robe. The cabby was saying something to him, and he was restlessly scanning the area with his eyes. What if he went to the water tower? No, he headed off to the side towards the long warehouse building. I whispered about this man to Yusup, we decided not to say anything to Kutbia, not to disturb her. When the train arrived, I ducked under the buffers, jumped into the carriage from the platform and opened the vestibule door on the opposite side – the door, fortunately, was not locked. Yusup and Kutbia entered and sat down on a bench in a dark corner.

It was a direct train to Tashkent. The third bell rang, the conductor's whistle trilled, the locomotive roared. "Write to me poste restante, Yusup, have a nice trip!" - "I'll write, thank you!" The train started moving, I jumped off on the move. I wasn't worried about the fate of the fugitives: there were three soldiers in the same compartment with them.

The cabbies had all gone away, only mine was waiting for me. The way back to the city was long, the cabbie was in no hurry. The full moon was shining, filling the open spaces with a strong blue light, and in the shadows the road ended, fell into darkness, and the freshness from the trees wafted towards me. I was half asleep on the tight seat. Suddenly the cabbie said mockingly:

— But the carriage with the locomotive never arrived.

"Yes, he didn't come," I responded.

— An important person left by train?

"Yes, he left by train," I confirmed with a challenge in my voice. "And tell me, who did you get out onto the platform with? A tall man in a silk robe. Who was he looking for?"

The cab driver did not answer right away; my question caught him off guard.

"I don't know," he said after a pause. "Just some stranger. He was looking for the main boss on the railroad."

The cab driver was lying, that was clear to me. They were looking for Kutbia. But now she was far away, and the three soldiers in the compartment... couldn't be reached, even if they went through the carriages. I grinned: keep looking, keep looking! But it was too early for me to grin – for her, for Yusup, it was all over, but for me it was just beginning.

I should have thought about the appearance of this man in a silk robe, about the cabbie's false answer, but I was brave in those years, or rather, careless. It never even occurred to me that Kutbia's relatives, having lost her, might turn their revenge on me. Another strange thing happened when entering Khodzhent: the cabbie flatly refused to go to the market square, to my teahouse, citing some urgent business at home. Then I realized: he was afraid that I would be stabbed in his carriage. But I didn't understand anything at first - I let him go and went on foot.

My teahouse was brightly lit by two pot-bellied lanterns, and as always, sellers of flatbreads, boiled lamb, beetroot sausage, and grapes were standing by the platform with their baskets. I bought one, and another, and a third, because I had not had lunch today. The teahouse owner handed me a teapot, handed it to me silently, without asking where I had been all day. And suddenly, at the far end of the teahouse, I saw the same man who had gone out onto the station platform with the cabby, wearing the same silk robe. Without finishing his teapot, he threw three kopecks onto the tray and went out. Only now did something scratch me in the heart. "But if he is following me, he would not have shown himself so openly," I thought reassuringly, and immediately realized: after all, he does not know that I saw him on the platform, that is why he is showing himself openly. Or maybe it was just a coincidence - a man just happened to walk into this teahouse, that's all.

No, it was not a simple coincidence. The teahouse owner, looking away, said that my overnight stays in his teahouse were over, that a new exorbitant tax had been set for overnight stays today and that I would have to leave. "You owe me a ruble sixty kopecks," the teahouse owner finished. He, too, was afraid that I would be stabbed in his teahouse. I left.

Now I knew for sure: I was being hunted. It was very strange to find myself in the position of a person being hunted. And the night, as luck would have it, was moonlit, making it easy for the enemies to spy on me.

Three streets and five alleys opened onto the market square, and an ambush could be waiting anywhere. And I didn't even have a stick in my hands. I returned to the teahouse, pulled a pole out from under the platform, broke it and armed myself. The teahouse owner said nothing, made a deaf ear, blind eyes. I again went back to the middle of the square.

Here I was exposed from all sides, but I could see in all directions. I imagined very clearly how they would find my body in the morning and no one would show any interest in this case, they would write a report at the police station, that's all. And they wouldn't even inform me at home, because the murderers would, of course, take all my papers. But where should I go, I can't stand all night in the square?.. And I can't stand and it's scary to leave: the alleys are tight, narrow, fenced off with blank fences, blind walls, there's nowhere to go.

I walked slowly toward the alley, the exit of which was lost in deep shadow. In my youth I had very keen eyesight, Kyrgyz eyesight, and my left pupil was elongated. During the day it was almost unnoticeable, but at night the pupil dilates twice as much as the right, and in my youth I, like a blind cat, could see with my left eye in the dark. And I noticed some movement in the alley. They! I had to lure them out. Turning sharply, I walked toward the street that was lit by the moon. And so it was - they, hiding behind the shadows, thinking that I did not see them, quickly walked toward the same street. They did not know that I had penetrated their plan through the cab driver and the teahouse owner, they were counting on my ignorance.

Here was the street close by, and they, the three of them, came out of the darkness to intercept me. I pretended not to suspect anything and walked forward, straight toward them. I recognized one, tall, in a silk robe, the other two were unknown to me.

And when only ten or twelve steps separated us and they had already prepared their knives under their robes, I suddenly ran to the alley from which I had lured them. They, stamping their boots, chased after me.

It's a tricky business to catch up with a man running away from death, I got ahead of them and was the first to burst into the alley, raising my stick just in case. No one, the way is clear. The dogs in the yards went crazy when they heard me, marking my path with their frantic barking. There, at the turn, the fence seemed lower than the others, and the dogs' barking could not be heard behind it, I darted over the fence like a fish and hid on the other side.

My pursuers raced past. The excited dogs were now barking all along the alley and all the neighboring alleys; more and more dogs were joining in, the whole of night Khojent was barking, howling, wheezing, choking and barking at the different dog voices.

But I had to look around – where did I end up? A mosque, that's what! I jumped into the courtyard of a small mosque, that's why there were no dogs here. And the guard? He must be asleep. At that moment he came out from behind the mosque into the courtyard, stopped, listened to the dogs barking, sat down on the sufa and dozed off, snoring softly. Praise be to Allah! – he didn't notice me in the shadows, under the fence…

About ten minutes later, voices were heard in the alley: my pursuers were returning.

- He probably ran to the Syr Darya...

- No, he turned towards the road to the station. We need to look for him there...

They passed, their voices died down. Now I knew that I couldn't show up at the station. Well, I'll leave on foot, along a country road.

…The early dawn lifted the fog over the land, awakening the first birds. And when I went out of town, into the fields and gardens, the sun was already rising, promising the world a clear and quiet day. The dew sparkled and glittered on the grass and leaves, muddy water ran towards me along the irrigation ditch, born in the mountains from a blue glacier just an hour ago. The night shadows went to the west, and with them my recent fears went away: three with knives, a chase in a narrow dark alley. But enough, did all this even happen?.. I regretted one thing - that I would not now learn about the further fate of Yusup and Kutbia, that the letters addressed to me in Khujand would remain lying in the post office, unclaimed by anyone.

"Green Prosecutor"

I arrived in Andizhan in the autumn; the last melons were already being picked from the melon fields and laid on flat roofs to ripen in the autumn sun, and in all the villages around the city the air was filled with a subtle fragrance. Autumn is the time of abundance, the time of gardens sagging under the weight of ripe fruit, with the pale pinkish yellow of peaches through the foliage, with the crimson-brick spots of large pomegranates. The rice fields in the lowlands sparkled with a dull, blinding expanse of water, the vineyards were empty, and only where the latest, sweetest bunches were slowly ripening, flocks of small birds flashed like a transparent net from morning to evening, and the drawn-out cries of guards and the frantic ringing of basins and buckets could be heard. These cries and ringing produced the desired effect on the starlings and thrushes, but none on the sparrows: the sparrows did not act in flocks, but each one alone, in a loose formation, causing indescribable losses to the owners of the vineyards. "Look!" the guard shouted indignantly, showing me a bunch of grapes pecked by the sparrows. "Look, look where he's climbing, the damned baigush[9], he doesn't need grapes, he needs the seeds from the middle, the seeds!" And the sparrows noisily and cheerfully fussed about in the foliage, chirped, fought, plucking feathers from each other, and the air, glassy, warmed by the sun, stood motionless, and in the distance above the earth a streaming haze trembled and floated...

On the outskirts of the city, on a huge vacant lot, a fair began to bustle. Its center was a racecourse, where horse games were held daily - "baiga", otherwise goat-slaying. A hundred horsemen lined up in a semicircle in front of a platform where judges sat. The carcass of a slaughtered goat was dragged out to the middle of the field. At a signal from the platform, the horsemen rushed in a tight crowd to the carcass. It was necessary to pick it up from the ground, throw it on the saddle, press it down with their feet, gallop three circles and throw the carcass in front of the platform. The winner was awarded a prize - a silk robe or embroidered, elegant ichigi - soft boots without heels.

The carnage began when the carcass was still lying on the ground. The riders yelled, waved their whips, neighed, collided, the

---

[9] *Baigush* is an outsider, a beggar, a vagabond, a person from a nomadic tribe.

110

horses reared up, kicked in the air with their front legs, hitting the riders, and woe to anyone who flew out of the saddle: they could be trampled in the general melee, beaten to death with hooves, and maimed - this was inevitable.

The scramble around the carcass was seething, the excitement, growing, was already transmitted to the horses, they neighed thinner, shriller, with anger, they reared up steeper, threatening to fall over onto their backs. The carcass was no longer lying down - it was hanging, it was being torn from each other by dozens of riders who had reached it first, the rest - latecomers - were making their way to it, furiously lashing with a heavy whip to the right and to the left, at the horses and at the riders indiscriminately. That is why there used to be so many crooked men in Central Asia. The scramble intensified, finally some horseman would seize the carcass and throw it onto the saddle, under his feet. But this did not mean victory, there were still three circles left. Rarely did a lucky man manage to break ahead, alone, usually three would break out: in the middle - a lucky man on a horse going at full gallop, and on the sides, level with him, at the same furious gallop - two rivals, hanging in the saddles, tightly, with ossified hands, clutching the carcass, ready to die rather than give in. Three horses walked closely, the rest rushed behind them in a tight disorderly bunch; the crowd surrounding the field roared and whooped in discord, and to the side, in the shadow, on white felts sat tabibs - Uzbek doctors-bone-setters and calmly awaited their hour. They did not have to wait long: two rivals, racing to the right and left, with their combined efforts lifted the carcass over the saddle, and along with it the rider, and he, having lost his stirrups, immediately flew to the ground and remained motionless. They picked him up and dragged him to the white blankets; now it was not three, but only two who were arguing for the carcass, the others managed to fly up, and again a fierce melee began to boil on the field. It also happened that the whole crowd of horsemen crashed into the crowd, and the spectators who did not have time to jump back were also carried to the white blankets - some with bloody heads, some with broken ribs.

And all around the fair was seething and bubbling - a whole nomadic town of reed mats that had sprung up on a vacant lot in one day. Teahouses, taverns, shops, market jesters-masqueraders[10],

---

[10] *Maskarabas* (maskharoboz) are folk actors who usually performed at weddings and other family celebrations.

tightrope walkers, Chinese magicians, Indian snake charmers, three-leaf and strap players, owners of penny roulettes.

I was pushing my way through the fair for a long time and suddenly I saw a booth made of the same reed mats, but larger than the others in size; there was a crowd of people in front of the booth, from time to time they all let out an enthusiastic roar, fell silent for a short time and let out a roar again. I approached, heard the weak dry clicks of shots - it was a shooting gallery. It remained unclear why the crowd in front of it was roaring so enthusiastically. Having pushed my way to the stand, I understood everything.

This was a special shooting gallery, indecent, only for men. The figures cut out of tin depicted women in long monastic robes; if a shot was successful, a ringing crack of a spring was heard, the robes fell, and the women appeared before the crowd completely naked, and they were painted very realistically. The target that was located further and higher than all enjoyed particular success; it depicted a moustached, bug-eyed man in a bowler hat and an oriental woman sitting opposite each other; if the shot hit the aiming circle, not only did the clothes fall from both of them, but the woman also sat on the man's lap. It was this frivolous scene that caused such delight in the crowd, accompanied by a powerful roar.

They were shooting with small Monte Cristo guns. I took five cartridges. One of my shots hit the target - the figures became naked, and the woman sat down on the man's lap. "O-o-o!" the crowd behind me howled and groaned, and the owner of the shooting gallery, not paying attention to the other shooters, rushed, bending over to the target, to set it up again before the spectators had time to look at it. Then I saw that the owner's thick wadded cap had a piece of boiler iron hanging from the back, covering the back of his head and neck. The owner was setting up the target, and all five guns continued to shoot; when he had finished his work, he, still bending over, ran to the stand, whistled by bullets from all sides.

"It might catch on," I said.

- Nothing complicated, - he answered. - It's my job. I went to the local museum and saw some old chain mail there. If only I had one like that, then nothing would bother me. But without the chain mail, it's a pain, of course.

"And deep?" I inquired.

- No, it only goes under the skin about three millimeters, but it's still unpleasant. However, the local paramedic deftly pulls them out, he has a special hook.

At this moment the crowd roared again, someone again hit the main target, and again the owner, bending down, rushed towards it, whistled at by bullets from all sides.

"Chainmail is not at all necessary," I said when he returned to the counter. "It can be simpler. Do you have an old quilted jacket?"

- Yes, but what's the point? I tried it - it works.

- I'll do it - it won't work.

The last box of cartridges had just run out, and the shooting range had to be closed until the next day.

The owner spent the night right there, in his hut. He got an old, greasy quilted jacket from the corner, I diluted salt brine[11] in a basin, spread the jacket on wooden forks and dipped my back into the basin. About three hours later I hung it out in the breeze to dry. By morning the jacket had dried, its back had acquired a wooden rigidity. We tried it – bullets did not penetrate the jacket from the back.

- Tell me, how simple, but try to figure it out! - the owner was surprised.

I already knew his name, patronymic and surname - Grigory Fedotovich Ksenofontov. He was over forty years old, and from under his broad, overhanging eyebrows his eyes looked out - not small, sharp, prickly, as one would expect from such eyebrows, but large, blue, clear eyes, from which it was immediately obvious that he was a kind and simple-hearted person. And he really was. When he went to town to get some cartridges, he entrusted me, a complete stranger, with guarding his shooting range. He came back worried.

- I got the last eight boxes from the hunting society. - He unloaded the cartridges from his pockets. - There are no more, and the season is just beginning. I'll have to go to Tashkent, get a hundred boxes.

Ten thousand cartridges! He expected to make a good profit at the fair.

- It won't be enough, - he calculated thoughtfully. - Autumn is dry, it will stand for about a month and a half. The main thing is that the targets are very attractive to the public. I saw how they shoot -

---

[11] *Salt brine* is water in bodies of water that is a saturated salt solution.

from all five Montecrist at once. If only the police don't cover it up. Well, yes, by the time they get together, the fair will be over. I'll take a hundred and fifty boxes, they won't go to waste. I think I'll go on the evening train today, and you'll manage here alone without me.

- What if I can't handle it, Grigory Fedotovich?

- Why? Nothing tricky, I saw it myself. Put a padded jacket on your shoulders, a hat with a piece of iron on your head, and off you go. You'll sell out these eight boxes in two days.

So I got a job at the shooting range on one-fifth of the income. This promised fifty to sixty rubles a month, that is an amount that more than covered all my needs at that time. I was responsible for servicing the shooters and cleaning the guns in the evenings. The risk of getting a bullet in the thigh three millimeters under the skin was included in this verbal agreement.

The train to Tashkent left at nine in the evening. Grigory Fedotovich shaved, changed into a tussoo suit, cleaned his dress straw hat with a brush and soap, and prepared his suitcase.

"Take a shovel and dig here, in this place," he said.

"Why?" I was surprised.

- Dig, since the master orders you.

I started digging and at the depth of two shovels I came across a tin box. Grigory Fedotovich's money was kept in it. He counted out the required amount and put it in his pocket.

- Now bury it.

"Grigory Fedotovich," I said with despair in my voice, "why did you show me this box, and right before leaving!"

- What, you don't rely on yourself? - he grinned. - But I do, I trust you.

- You only know me from yesterday. Maybe I'm some kind of crook, a thief?

- You are as far from a regular thief, who is within the law, as from the sky, - Grigory Fedotovich said impressively. - You are not the right breed. You are also not fit to be a crook due to your weak character. Trample the earth, level the earth, so that it is not noticeable.

- You'd better put your money in the book. He stopped me sternly.

- And this is none of your business. Listen here. There is a note in the box about the money - where to put it in case something happens to me. Got it?

- What could happen to you?

— Different things happen.

And he went to the station, leaving me to worry about the box of money. I did worry, I kept wondering if anyone had peeped through the crack in the booth when I was digging and burying it. At about three in the morning I got up and went outside. The late autumn dawn had not yet begun, the fair was sleeping without lights, in silence. A breeze was blowing, cold, sharp, with a reminder of the coming winter. The ridge of poplars bordering the fair was visible darkly and uniformly, and in the sky above it the stars were burning, already bright as in winter. And there was not a soul around. I returned to the booth, dug a hole in another place, hid the box. It was safer that way, better, no one could pee.

In the morning my work began, in a hat with a piece of iron hanging on the back, in a padded jacket with a wooden back, I, just like Grigory Fedotovich, ran bent over, hearing the thin squeak of bullets above me.

Two days later Grigory Fedotovich returned with cartridges, he returned gloomy, worried about something. He hardly spoke to me, left the booth in the morning, came back in the evening, silently accepted the money, without counting it. Some kind of melancholy that I did not understand stood in his eyes like dark water. I did not ask, he gratefully appreciated my restraint. We lived silently, but amicably.

Three weeks passed. During this time I still caught one bullet in my leg three millimeters under the skin and went to the paramedic, learned his terrible hook. But otherwise our shooting range worked briskly, the income grew.

All this was interrupted in the most unexpected way - one morning, before the shooting range opened, two policemen came to our booth, one Russian, with a revolver on his side, and the other Uzbek, with a rifle.

"Hello to you," said the Russian. "Who's the owner?"

- I am the owner. - Grigory Fedotovich stepped forward. - You mean about the targets? Well, nothing special, citizen chief. Now if I showed the obscene cards in a stereoscope, like the others at the fair, then it would be understandable. But the targets are tin...

- What other targets, - answered the policeman. - We are on another matter. So, you are the boss. What is your full name?

"What is it?" Grigory Fedotovich did not understand.

- Full name. Well, last name, first name, patronymic. What? Ksenofontov Grigory Fedotovich... Or maybe another full name? - A slow smile pulled at the policeman's thick lips. - For example, Pavlov Ivan Maksimovich.

Never have I seen a person change so much in a second. Grigory Fedotovich (or Ivan Maksimovich - now I didn't know what to call him) turned a dull yellow and was silent for a long time, without a drop of blood in his face. The policeman also remained expectantly silent.

"Well," Grigory Fedotovich finally said. "You win. Let's go…"

At the exit from the booth he turned to me.

- Keep an eye here. Don't forget about the note I ordered you to.

"What note?" the policeman asked sternly.

"Yes, this is to record the number of cartridges fired," I helped out the owner.

"That's possible," said the policeman. "Go ahead, write it down!"

And they left - Grigory Fedotovich in the middle, with his hands behind his back, one policeman in front, the second, with a rifle at the ready, behind.

Arrested... For what, for what crime? But Grigory Fedotovich was expecting this arrest, that's why he was so gloomy, anxious, silent with me. That's why he told me about the box with money, about the note in it. Then I realized - there was no search, they could come back, search the booth! I grabbed a shovel, quickly dug up the box, took out the money, the note. I counted it - one thousand one hundred thirty-eight rubles in large bills of three, five and ten chervonets. The note contained a request to give the money to Pavlova Galina Mikhailovna, city of Buzuluk, Sovetskaya Street, house 19. So, that's right, in fact he is Pavlov, not Ksenofontov. Married and disappeared from Buzuluk. What could he have done in Buzuluk?

I buried the empty box back in the hole, stamped the earth, locked the booth, put the key in a designated place known only to the two of us, and left with someone else's money in my pocket.

It was not in vain, it was not in vain that I reproached Grigory Fedotovich - why did he tell me about his box, about the note. How good it would be not to know anything about them! I wandered around Andijan, and other people's money was burning me. At first I wanted to go straight to the post office and transfer it by telegraph to Buzuluk to Galina Mikhailovna. Then I changed my mind: the money could be intercepted, if not here, then in Buzuluk - it is not for nothing that he writes "transfer" and not "forward". Damn it, do I really have to go to Buzuluk? There, probably, there is already snow, and I do not have a winter coat, a hat, or felt boots. Let's say that all this can be bought with this same money, since the trip to Buzuluk is being undertaken for the sake of Galina Mikhailovna... Here my thoughts were distracted: it would be very effective to send a telegram home to Kokand from Buzuluk - look, as if to say, where I have ended up! But maybe they are already looking for me? Maybe they searched and found an empty box? No, how could they know about it? Or maybe Grigory Fedotovich showed it during interrogation? After all, then they will consider me a thief!

This thought stunned me to the point of weakness in the knees, to a disgusting emptiness in the stomach. What to do? But he said: "In case something happens." Of course, he meant arrest, he was counting on me and he wouldn't say anything during the interrogation.

Why should I become a harborer of a criminal, his accomplice? Perhaps he is a murderer! But I remembered his clear blue eyes under his shaggy overhanging eyebrows, his constant benevolent evenness in his treatment of me - such people are not murderers. Stole a large sum? But he did not steal one thousand one hundred and thirty-eight rubles, it was not worth getting dirty for such money. And why did he need a shooting gallery, why was he so concerned about his money, so that it would be given to his wife? That is how one cares about the last and only money, and not about some side money.

In my anxious thoughts I didn't even notice how I had wandered into the old city. It was Wednesday, market day, sellers and buyers had come to Andijan from all over the area on carts, horses, donkeys, camels, the bazaar was already noisy, crowded and agitated. But I saw and heard everything as if from afar, completely absorbed in my thoughts.

I must admit that the voice of civil and state conscience was silent in me - or rather, it was drowned out by the powerful sound of the eleventh commandment: "Do not inform." God, of course, wrote such a commandment on the tablets, but Moses scraped out God's word, since he was a statesman. I did not go to the police, wandered around the old city all day, and in the evening I went to the fair to see whether our booth had been searched or not.

Even from afar I saw the open door of the booth. But I had locked the door. That meant there had been a search. Perhaps there were policemen sitting in the booth right now, waiting for me. But why did they leave the door open? They weren't such fools as to warn me of their ambush with an open door.

I looked at the booth from afar for a long time. Everything around it was quiet, empty, although the rest of the fair was still noisy. Maybe the policemen simply left after the unsuccessful search, without closing the door through carelessness?

With endless precautions, hiding behind the reed tents, looking around at every step, I approached the booth, looked through a crack. And I was immensely surprised to see Grigory Fedotovich Ksenofontov - Ivan Maksimovich Pavlov. He was sitting on a stool, drinking moonshine from a bottle, snacking on bread and tomatoes. He was alone in the booth, completely alone. The money box lay in front of him on the counter, next to the bottle.

- Grigory Fedotovich! - I called quietly. He jumped up and shouted joyfully:

- Well, go, go, don't be afraid! There's no one!

I entered the booth and, immediately turning pale, placed Grigory Fedotovich's money on the counter in front of him.

"Take it," I said in a voice trembling with resentment. "And never again entrust me with any of your money, I don't want to have anything to do with it... You are deigning to walk around in the company of policemen, and I have to go to Buzuluk, to take your money to Galina Mikhailovna!"

I don't know why I was so offended, apparently the release after a whole day of unbearable tension poured out in me as an unconscious resentment. Grigory Fedotovich understood me that way.

- Now I'll go to Buzuluk myself, - he said seriously. - And you're wrong to be offended, because when they took me away, I thought - it's the end. I didn't expect to get out free. But now I've got out, and clean. Do you understand now?

And he showed me a paper from the police with a round seal. The paper said that comrade Pavlov Ivan Maksimovich, in accordance with the decision of the Supreme Court of the RSFSR, was released from prison as a person wrongly convicted.

I didn't understand anything. If so, why did they take him away in the morning? From what prisons was he being released if he had lived at large until now? Grigory Fedotovich (aka Ivan Maksimovich) was saying in the meantime:

- Tomorrow we won't be trading at the shooting range. You'll have other work. You need to treat the policemen for their fairness, for their efforts. You need to treat them well, so that they remember Ivan Maksimovich, the kind of person he is!..

That night we did not sleep until dawn. Ivan Maksimovich told me his fate. He told it slowly, dwelling on all the details. Truly, such amazing stories do not happen often and, according to the Eastern expression, are worthy of being written down "with the point of a needle in the corner of the eye." I am conveying this story here in my own words.

After finishing the civil war, Ivan Maksimovich returned to his family in Buzuluk. In 1924, he was appointed by promotion to the TPO - Transport Consumer Society - and was put in charge of four siding cars - shops for railway workers on the line.

The farm was not very large, and Ivan Maksimovich managed it strictly, but the inspection that came six months later found that many boxes of candy, cookies, pasta, many sacks of granulated sugar and twenty-seven poods of sausage were missing.

Ah, this sausage - how many people it has ruined!.. A man lives, without a single stain on his conscience, blamelessly went through the revolution, through the civil war, and then the teasing, garlicky smell of sausage hit him in the nose - and he was lost, tempted, ruined! That's probably what the auditors thought when they drew up their report, according to which Ivan Maksimovich was threatened with the dock. He himself knew that he was not involved in these disappearances, in twenty-seven poods of sausage, but try to explain, prove where it all actually went.

Ivan Maksimovich was a newbie in trade, he didn't understand anything about the various tricks that seasoned businessmen had studied to the last detail. He didn't know, for example, that sausage brought from the warehouse should not be put on sale immediately, but should be kept overnight under damp sacks, and by morning it would gain weight due to the moisture it had absorbed - then you could trade, counting the difference into your pocket. The same simple trick can be done with granulated sugar, and for sweets there is another trick, for example, tearing off the labels from the boxes and selling the second grade for the first, for vegetable oil - the third, and so on, for each product - its own trick, not counting the tricks of universal application, like an electric fan: it works very well if you direct the air stream from it to the scale pan - eighty grams are cleaned from each weight, and in a day, look, and it has accumulated ... Experienced businessmen with indescribable dexterity perform their acquisitive suites on the polyphonic instrument of fraud and are caught extremely rarely. But for a new person, trading is always a trap!

And Ivan Maksimovich ended up on trial for the sins of others. When the investigation was underway, he wrote to his former civil war commissar in Moscow. Now this commissar was in high rank and held a high position, but he responded to the letter of the old Red Army soldier and came to Buzuluk. He arrived just the day after the verdict, according to which Ivan Maksimovich had to go to a correctional labor camp for three years, with a loss of rights.

The Moscow guest got a meeting with Ivan Maksimovich. He entered the cell, did not shake hands. He sat down on a stool. And Ivan Maksimovich stood in front of him with his head down.

- How about you? - asked the Moscow guest. - How did it turn out so badly, Ivan Maksimovich?

- I don't know, citizen commissar. - After the sentence, Ivan Maksimovich no longer had the right to address free people with the word "comrade", he was specially warned about this. - I only know that I didn't take any cookies, candies, or sausage. And where it went, who took it, I don't know.

- Can you swear that you didn't take it? - asked the Moscow guest. - Remember, I carried you out of the battle wounded in my arms and through you I myself received a shrapnel in the lower back. By your blood, by my blood, can you swear a terrible bloody oath?

Ivan Maksimovich immediately remembered that battle with the Dutovites near the Kuvandyk station, between Orenburg and Orsk, how pure he was then before everyone, it would have been better if he had been killed in that battle, the bullet would have hit lower, right in the heart. Tears welled up in Ivan Maksimovich's eyes. But the Moscow guest was waiting for an answer.

- I swear, Comrade Commissar, by my blood and yours, shed together on the battlefield, I am not guilty of anything, I have not used a single kopeck! I swear by a terrible oath!

The policeman accompanying the Moscow guest turned away, hiding his excitement.

The Moscow guest extended his hand to Ivan Maksimovich.

- I believe you! Since you swore, I believe you. And you believe me, Ivan Maksimovich, go to the camp calmly, and I'll be here without you, trying to figure it out. And I'll figure it out, I promise! I won't leave until I figure it out!..

Ivan Maksimovich ended up in one of the camps in the north. A month passed, then a second - he still hoped, waited for a letter from the commissar. A third month passed, then a fourth - and hope faded in his soul.

And just then Ivan Maksimovich was transferred to another camp point. They showed him a place on the bunks in the barracks. His bunkmates, to the right and to the left, were two thieves, both of them law-abiding, with rights, representatives of the prison-camp aristocracy. They greeted Ivan Maksimovich very unfriendly. Seizing a moment, he approached the warden.

- Citizen chief, why did you put me among the thieves? I feel offended.

- Offended? - the warden narrowed his eyes. - And how are you better?..

Just three words, and they killed Ivan Maksimovich outright. Indeed, how is he better than these thieves in the eyes of those around him? Who here knows about his innocence, who will believe him, if in the camp everyone, except the thieves, claims that they are innocent and are sitting in vain. And they are despised for this by the thieves, who openly and even proudly talk about their dark exploits and even exaggerate them in order to rise above themselves. "And how are you better?" said the warden, and quite rightly so, because the sentence for Ivan Maksimovich included theft of cooperative property. After these words, Ivan Maksimovich became embittered, decided to himself: "If I am not better than the thieves, then I will be the same as them, life is ruined anyway..."

He remembered his former commissar with a nasty smile: he had backed down, abandoned him in trouble, the same scoundrel, self-loving person as all people. In these thoughts about the commissar, in this loss of trust in people, lay his gravest sin, in comparison with which all other minor sins could not be taken into account at all.

On the fronts of the civil war, Ivan Maksimovich was characterized by desperation in battles, so that at times it was even necessary to restrain him. Then, in peaceful days, this desperation died down, but here, at the turning point in the camp, it flared up again.

Ivan Maksimovich understood that it was not so easy to get along with thieves; he had to stand out in some way, distinguish himself, otherwise the thieves would not accept him.

And he distinguished himself, stood out - with desperate, ugly violations of camp rules. He was invariably put in a punishment cell, on a penalty ration, he did not give in, he began to misbehave again.

One day the head of the camp called him.

"What do you want, Pavlov?" he asked. "What are you trying to achieve? After all, I can see that you are not what you seem, not at all."

Ivan Maksimovich paused, thought, and unexpectedly responded to the chief with a waterfall of the most disgusting camp obscenities, while he tried to shout as loudly as possible, with the goal that the prisoner on duty in the corridor would hear him and that through the prisoner on duty the rumor would spread throughout the camp about his desperation in the conversation with the chief and reach the thieves.

He achieved his goal. He was taken straight from the office to the punishment cell, but the rumor of his desperation in the conversation with the chief spread throughout the camp and reached the thieves.

In the end, the thieves allowed him into their company, although not on equal terms, but they did allow him in. He religiously observed the thieves' code: not to work, not to accept any camp positions, even the most advantageous ones, such as foreman, bread cutter or foreman, to speak to the authorities only in obscene words, to despise and oppress "fraers", that is, everyone outside the tight circle of thieves, with the exception of priests and artists, whom the thieves considered their younger brothers.

Meanwhile, spring was approaching - a time of anxiety, a time of escape.

It is known that in spring every person is drawn to some indefinite distance. A prisoner is drawn ten times more strongly, and to a very definite distance - beyond the high, sharp palisade, to freedom.

The famous escape of the old thief Vasily Parfenovich was still alive and glorious in the memory of the camp inmates, and a song about this escape was still being sung to the guitar. This is how it began:

When the "green prosecutor"[12]
He signed my release...
And again I came out into the open,
I saw the awakening of life,
I saw a solid carpet of grass,
Covered with lush flowers,
And I cried, old thief,
With big, big tears...

Vasily Parfenovich did cry - thieves, as is well known, are extremely sensitive people, it is not for nothing that each of them has blue inscriptions on their chest: "I will not forget my mother" and "There is no happiness in life" - he did cry, but nevertheless, in his escape, he burned down the forest village of Shaly, notorious in the criminal world for its ostentatious hospitality to fugitives, with their subsequent surrender to the cordon for two poods of flour, eight pounds of herring and thirty rubles in cash for each head handed over. So the Shaly people tried, until the hand of fate, which this time took the form of old Vasily Parfenovich, fell on their own heads.

He had his own scores to settle with this village: it was from here that he had been taken to the cordon during his previous unsuccessful escape, two years ago. This time Vasily Parfenovich did not approach the village openly, but crept up, hiding in the bushes. He waited until nightfall. As luck would have it, the night was dark and windy, the first spring thunderstorm was slowly and heavily coming from the east, distant lightning blazed, palely illuminating the horizon, and the distant dull rumble of thunder could be heard. Vasily Parfenovich approached from the windward side and set fire to last year's straw in four places, they caught fire, fiery jackdaws flew towards the village,

---

[12] The words "green prosecutor" mean spring.

setting the straw roofs on fire, and when a rainstorm approached with a thunderstorm three hours later, he had only firebrands to douse.

The song said it like this:
And until the morning with a big fire
Those vile huts were burning,
And screams were heard all around,
And the children screamed loudly.
There was a pine forest all around
And he echoed the cry with a resounding echo,
And I laughed, the old thief,
For his revenge with cruel laughter.

Ivan Maksimovich, together with the thieves, enthusiastically sang this camp song to the tune of "Ermak". True, at night he often heard an inner voice: "What are you doing, Ivan Maksimovich, come to your senses, you are an honest working man, and the thieves - they are bastards, bastards, enemies of working people." But this voice was drowned out by the voice of bitterness: "Oh, I am no better, I will be the same!.."

For yet another act of art, he - for the umpteenth time! - ended up in a punishment cell, in a cell where three thieves were sitting. They started playing cards. The warden saw through the peephole and opened the door.

"Give me the cards!" he said sternly.

"What cards?" the short, dark-haired Mitka Ugolyok, a pickpocket, still very young but already in his element, responded in an innocent voice.

- Are you seeing things, chief? The warden called two more warders, the three of them conducted the most thorough, most complete search of the cell, examined every crack and found nothing.

Looking through the peephole ten minutes later, the warden again saw a card game. He entered, searched the entire cell again, this time alone, and again was left with nothing.

I looked through the peephole ten minutes later - they were playing!..

He came in and said:

- Well, to hell with you, finish the game, demons, I won't interfere. Just show me where you hide the cards?

To general laughter, Mitka Ugolek took the cards out of the warden's own jacket, from the side pocket. Then, laughing at himself, the warden went out and locked the cell, leaving its inhabitants to finish the game.

And that game was not simple, it was a game of escape. According to the sacred and immutable thieves' laws, the three losers were obliged to arrange an escape for the fourth, the winner, at least at the cost of their own heads. Ivan Maksimovich won the escape. It happened late in the evening, after lights out. In accordance with the agreement, they gave the cards to the warden and went to bed on the bunks. But no one could sleep.

The thieves couldn't sleep because of their loss, but Ivan Maksimovich, on the contrary, couldn't sleep because of his unexpected luck. Having won the escape and realized his win, its significance, he became scared. Until now, he had been hanging out with the thieves as if it were a joke, but now he was tying himself firmly to them.

This is exactly how the "tolkoviche" - the general meeting of all the legal thieves held in the camp - understood this winning. At the beginning of the tolkoviche, a question arose: are all the thieves in law obliged to help a half-fraier who does not have thief's rights to escape? It was decided that they may not help the half-fraier himself, that is, Ivan Maksimovich, but they are obliged to help their comrades who lost in preparing the escape, and therefore, through them, they are obliged to help the half-fraier. Of course, the thieves in law should not have accepted a half-fraier into such a serious game, but that is another matter for which the losing thieves are responsible, and the winning half-fraier must get his in full.

Having thus overcome the difficulties in interpreting the law, the meeting moved on to discussing a detailed escape plan on three points: preparation, place and time. They discussed it slowly, in a businesslike manner, taking into account absolutely everything: the weather, possible escape routes, the personal characteristics of the guards on duty, and especially the imminent arrival of detective dogs at the camp. The latter circumstance greatly concerned the thieves, and they decided that the escape should take place no later than a week later, before the dogs arrived.

Listening to the debate at the meeting, Ivan Maksimovich understood: the way back was closed, he could not refuse to escape, as he, by the way, was thinking about: they would consider it base cowardice, betrayal, they would deal with him in their own way, with

125

knives. Now he would inevitably soon have to switch to the wolfish life of a fugitive.

It has been noted that any group of shady criminals strives to lure and entangle more people from the outside into their crimes - this way the shady people can live more peacefully. Having entangled Ivan Maksimovich, the thieves were filled with a firm determination to bring the matter to a successful conclusion. The leader of the thieves' company, Pyotr Evdokimovich, an old thief, gave him the address of a "raspberry" in Syzran and a password known only to a few.

- There they will fix you a linden tree, - said Pyotr Evdokimovich, - well, and they will give you some money, and you go from Syzran somewhere far away, at least to Irkutsk. There you will go to Privokzalnaya, thirty-three, ask for Mikhail Semenovich Gavrilov - he is one of our own. Give him greetings from Taras Timofeevich Paley, and he will ask you whether Taras has moved from Novorossiysk to Tuapse or is still in Novorossiysk? When he asks about this, start a direct conversation and then stick with Gavrilov: he will put you to work, to our work, because now you have only one path left - with us ...

Ivan Maksimovich listened, and his heart ached quietly: Pyotr Evdokimovich's words were like a funeral bell for him. Farewell, honest life, farewell forever! Eh, Ivan Maksimovich, Ivan Maksimovich, where has stubborn resentment led you!

- Don't go home, don't show your face! - continued Pyotr Evdokimovich. - Where do they catch fugitives who are inexperienced? Most of them are at home. He circles and circles and knows that he can't go home, but he still comes. He's drawn like a magnet... And there they wait for him, my dear fellow, take him and add to his sentence. But they rarely catch a fugitive thief. Why? Because he has no home. Forget about your family completely. You don't have a family now and you never will. If you get caught, they'll add to your sentence, and you'll be without a family; if you don't get caught, you'll be without a family again. Either way, you've lost your family forever. It's better, I tell you, in our business a family is of no use, it's nothing but a hassle and a burden, but in our business a person must be light and fast.

"First they read the funeral service for me, and now they're reading the funeral service for my family," flashed through Ivan

Maksimovich's mind. But he kept quiet: he was no longer his own master, his fate was being controlled by thieves.

They removed Ivan Maksimovich from the preparations for the escape completely, so that the guards would not have any suspicions about him. Everything was done without him: crackers were dried, shag was ground into a caustic dust to cover up traces in case the dogs arrived, something else was done, but Ivan Maksimovich did not really know what.

On the evening of May Day, a reinforced guard detail took over the duty. "It's time!" the thieves decided; the number of guards didn't bother them - it was even better if there were more guards.

In the morning, at about four o'clock, Ivan Maksimovich changed into the guard's uniform prepared by the thieves and went to the guardhouse. The thieves were watching from afar, from behind the dining room. Trembling all over, beside himself with fear, Ivan Maksimovich knocked on the window. The guard on duty raised his tousled head from the table and asked sleepily:

- What do you want?

"Let me out, Gubanov," Ivan Maksimovich said in a weak, alien voice. "My brother is coming to see me today, I need to tell the woman to slaughter the goose. I'll be back for roll call."

"Well, don't be late," said the guard on duty and pulled the iron bolt that locked the door. Ivan Maksimovich went out. "We got away with it!" the thieves whispered to each other.

Ah, how Ivan Maksimovich hoped that they would recognize him at the guard post and not let him go! They didn't recognize him, but they let him go. The escape was a success because it was conceived simply. Escapes with complicated plans almost always end in failure: too many separate parts must work together flawlessly for success. But here there were only two parts: the guard's uniform and the guard on duty, Gubanov - a damp, sleepy, stupid man who thought only of his three boars.

Once behind the guard, Ivan Maksimovich was already a fugitive, and anyone he met could shoot at him. Now, to save his life, he had to leave as quickly as possible, as far from the camp as possible.

Ivan Maksimovich rushed straight to the narrow-gauge railway. He was lucky, a train soon caught up with him - a dozen small platforms loaded with timber. He jumped on one of the platforms, the gray-moustached conductor looked at him tiredly and angrily from the platform, but said nothing. By eight o'clock in the morning Ivan Maksimovich was already far from the camp and was not going to leave the train, hoping to ride with it to the main line itself. He had calculated correctly - they would look for him in the forest, along the ravines, ravines, and caches, but it would not even occur to anyone to look for him on the railway, where everything is open to the eye. And in the camp, by now, there was probably already an alarm, the morning roll call had already taken place, they had already missed him, they were already announcing a search. Ivan Maksimovich smiled: they would search around the camp, in the forest, to a depth of ten to twelve miles—he would not be able to go further on foot—and by train he had already traveled sixty miles, and by lunch he would travel another sixty miles, and from there it was just a stone's throw to the highway, to the trains to Moscow.

He had already become accustomed to his new position as a fugitive, he was no longer afraid, on the contrary, he felt a desperate joy within himself and even sang a camp song to the sound of the wheels:

When the "green prosecutor"

He signed my release...

He felt a little intimidated on the main line, at the station: they could be waiting for him there. But it was unlikely – too little time had passed for him to get out onto the main line. But he had!.. He decided to behave openly, boldly – he stood in line at the ticket office, bought a ticket to Penza, intending to get off earlier, in Syzran. Everything worked out very well, and an hour later he was riding on a long-distance train and looking out of the vestibule for the last time at these deadly places here.

They didn't catch him. He didn't know one thing: they didn't catch him because they didn't try to catch him. In the camp, they did indeed miss one person during the roll call, and they raised the alarm, but they didn't get around to declaring a search. Just at the moment when the chief took up the pen to sign the search order, Ivan Maksimovich's former commissar entered the office and placed on the chief's desk a decision of the Supreme Court of the RSFSR, according to which Ivan Maksimovich was declared innocent of anything, and all the blame for the shortage of candies, cookies, granulated sugar, pasta, and twenty-seven poods of sausage was shifted to the warehouse manager, who admitted to forging the invoices.

The boss read the decision carefully and asked:

— Why was it not delivered in the usual way, but through you?

- I specifically asked in Moscow to be trusted to deliver this. Pavlov is my former Red Army soldier from the civil war, I want to personally meet him here and bring him home.

The boss thought about it, his cigarette went out.

— I can only help you with one thing: note that this decision was received yesterday, and the office was not working due to the holiday, which is why there was a delay.

"Why is this necessary?" asked the visitor.

- And then, between three and five o'clock in the morning, Pavlov escaped.

The visitor's mouth dropped open in surprise.

"If the paper is marked with today's date, then he should be given an additional term for escape, regardless of the acquittal in the main case," the chief explained. "But if it is marked with yesterday's date, then it turns out that Pavlov did not escape, but simply left the camp, having the right to do so. He left without documents, but that is his business."

- An amazing case! - said the visitor. - And a very offensive case for me. After all, I gave him my word that I would not back down until I sorted out his case. And he, go figure, ran away. That means he didn't believe me.

"He hung out with some bad people here, it was hard for him to keep his faith," the camp commander responded.

- Where can we look for him now?

- It's simple, - said the chief. - Go straight from here to his home in Buzuluk. Leave a copy of the court decision and a letter at home saying that there's no need for you to hide, you've been sent. He'll definitely drop by the house, they all come home like that in the end.

That's what they decided: the newcomer went to Buzuluk, and from there to Moscow, to his service.

And Ivan Maksimovich had already reached Syzran by this time, received a fake, one hundred and fifty rubles in money, and headed to Irkutsk, for another "raspberry".

Meanwhile, in the camp they learned that he had escaped, already being free, but not knowing it. The leader of the thieves, Pyotr Evdokimovich, darkened his face and said:

- It's high time to "sew" him now, otherwise, when he finds out, he can give away both "raspberries", both in Irkutsk and in Syzran. How many times have I told you, scoundrels, not to get involved in such a game with suckers! - he added, turning to Mitka Ugolko.

On the same day, letters from Pyotr Evdokimovich flew to Syzran and Irkutsk with urgent advice to "sew up," that is, kill, Ivan Maksimovich.

The letter arrived in Syzran after he had already left. But Irkutsk, also a mortal place, was waiting ahead. And Ivan Maksimovich would not have lost his head if he had not been drawn with an irresistible force to home. Although he knew that he could not go home, he could not resist. At the Kinel station, he left the Siberian train, transferred to the Tashkent train and got off in Buzuluk.

He made his way through the backs of his street, through the vegetable gardens to his house and hid in the raspberry patch. God forbid anyone should experience what he experienced when his wife Galina Mikhailovna came out into the yard, followed by her son and daughter. They sat down at a table in the shade to drink tea, and he lay in the raspberry patch, thirty steps away, and could neither get up nor raise his voice. Then Galina Mikhailovna went to the market with a basket, and the children ran to the neighbors' children, Ivan Maksimovich entered the empty familiar yard, put a note on the table - that, they say, he had been and gone on his way, therefore now he is a fugitive, forget me, and pressed the note with a flat stone so that the wind would not blow it away. A cat came out of the shed - the same old cat, recognized his owner, came to his feet and purred. Ivan Maksimovich took the cat in his arms, kissed its cold, wet nose, and thought to himself with unspeakable bitterness: "Well, I have to kiss the cat instead of my wife and children."

And he went to the station pale, with wet eyes. On the way to the station everything turned upside down in his soul, and he decided not to go to Irkutsk, not to take the thieves' road, but to go somewhere beyond Tashkent, and there, in a new place, to live honestly, although under a false name.

But why did he have to live under a false name, if at home, behind the altar, a package from the commissar was waiting for him?

Thirty steps, only thirty steps, was he from his happiness and freedom. And he did not walk these last thirty steps, he lay in the raspberry bush, did not make a sound...

And Galina Mikhailovna, returning home from the market, saw the note, read it and, of course, rushed straight to the police.

An all-Union search was announced, an amazing, unusual search, with the goal of returning the fugitive not to prison, but to freedom. This search caused a lot of talk among the police and agents. They were amazed, shrugged their shoulders, threw up their hands, but searched with tripled zeal: everyone was flattered to fulfill such a rare and amazing task.

Buzuluk is located on a railway line that forks further and leads along the main line to Tashkent, and along the side line to Guryev. It was correct to assume that Ivan Maksimovich would move to Tashkent, where there is incomparably more space than in Guryev. But he could also move back to Samara, and from there - the road to all ends ... A very troublesome and difficult matter - an all-Union search!

Thousands of people were looking for Ivan Maksimovich, but he was hiding. At first he wanted to get a job as a mechanic at the depot at Arys station, but they gave him a questionnaire to fill out. And suddenly this very questionnaire, which he would have filled out without any effort before, turned its sinister face to him. The name was alien, false, which meant that all the answers had to be false by necessity, which meant he had to invent other parents, another family, another whole life, and for everything to match up exactly. Without filling out the questionnaire, Ivan Maksimovich left Arys.

And the All-Union search worked - persistently, quietly, unnoticed by outsiders. Ivan Maksimovich wandered around various Central Asian cities, not staying anywhere for fear of being caught, until he got to Andijan. Here the line of his life crossed with the line of the All-Union search - he was identified, discovered, taken before my eyes and taken to the police. There he was first congratulated on his acquittal, and then scolded for a long time for the troubles and expenses caused to the All-Union search.

This is the story he told me that night. The next day he treated the policemen and, tipsy, sang to the guitar:

When the "green prosecutor"

He signed my release...

The policemen soon left. I asked Ivan Maksimovich:

— Did you send a telegram to Galina Mikhailovna in Buzuluk?
He grinned slyly.

- And I, without a telegram. In person.

- How so? - I said. - After all, she cried for three extra days.

"Or maybe there are no tears," he answered. "That's why I want to know if she's been faithful all this time without me or unfaithful."

He surprised me immensely with these words. So much for your blue, clear eyes! What thoughts a person carries within himself!

"I only saw her for a quarter of an hour, and that was from a distance," he said. "Now I'll look at her up close and find out..."

Having just been released from the search, he himself began his own, marital search. He had already forgotten everything: the raspberry patch and his tears thirty steps from home. So I learned that human memory sometimes has the property of being very short and that sudden happiness in other cases awakens in a person not only nobility.

I couldn't hide my thoughts, and I didn't want to.

We parted coldly.

Ivan Maksimovich sold his shooting range to some puny little man with weak eyes and protruding ears, well, a real bat! When the train started moving, taking Ivan Maksimovich to Buzuluk, I went to the telegraph office and sent Galina Mikhailovna a telegram: "Meet your husband on such and such a date, on such and such a train, in such and such a carriage, congratulations, your friend."

Having thus destroyed Ivan Maksimovich's insidious plans regarding his wife, I came to the shooting range the next morning.

The new owner was drinking tea. The targets were already set up, the guns were lying on the rack.

"Hello," I said.

"I don't need any help," he replied. "Let me give you the cold shoulder, young man."

In the semi-darkness of the closed booth he looked even more like a bat.

"My things are still here, my hat and my quilted jacket," I said.

"Take it," he replied. "I don't need such junk."

I silently took the hat with a piece of iron hanging from the back, the quilted jacket with a salted back and went out.

About fifteen minutes later the shooting range opened and shots started to click. The new owner was running under the bullets, unprotected. I waited patiently, not taking part in the shooting myself. Suddenly the new owner sat down, clutching the right side of his face with his hand.

He was shot through the right ear. He looked at his bloody fingers and screamed in a thin voice:

- Don't shoot, devils, stop shooting!

But the main target was still there, the shooting was intensifying, a spring clanged, clothes fell, a woman sat on a man's lap. The crowd howled, groaned... I left, taking with me a hat with a piece of iron, a salted quilted jacket, vindictively thinking that now the paramedic with a hook would have more work.

Now there are no more nomads in the country, the entire population has switched to a settled life, even the gypsies.

But earlier, during the years of the NEP, there were a great many nomads. Kirghiz, Cossacks, Beluchis[13], and Gypsies roamed the mountains and steppes, and the unemployed roamed the cities - several million unemployed, several million destitute, the always hungry stepchildren of life.

Socialism was only a dream then. "From each according to his ability, to each according to his work." But there was nowhere for a person to apply his abilities and nowhere to receive according to his work. Many did not even believe in socialism, considering it utopian propaganda.

That's how it was, exactly that way!

I live in Leningrad now, in an industrial city. There are notices on all the streets: "The plant requires stokers, turners, fitters of all grades, electricians, loaders, watchmen, guards, handymen, typists for the office, a secretary-typist with experience for the chief engineer's office." And the most amazing thing is that people are not surprised, they pass by without even reading: everyone has no time, everyone has their own business.

Everyone has their own business, just think about it! If such an announcement had appeared during the NEP times, there would have been no end to the inexhaustible flow of people pouring into the plant. The checkpoint would have been destroyed - that's how! Because they valued work, because it was not easy, and not for everyone and not right away, but only after a long search and half-starved wanderings. Therefore, having received a job, a person clung to it with both hands and even teeth...

Recently, our house committee tried an eagle - a twenty-six-year-old red-faced guy. In 1960 he changed six jobs and never worked anywhere for more than three weeks. In court, he was asked: why? He got stubborn: the work is unsuitable, my qualifications do not allow it, I have high painting qualifications, I want to paint doors in oak and paper offices with embossed "gravitol" wallpaper, which is cut and

---

[13] The Balochs are a people living in various Asian countries, their main occupations were nomadic cattle breeding and agriculture.

adjusted on glass with a steel ruler, but they let me paste ordinary wallpaper and even make me whitewash the ceilings - is that even possible?!

He spoke with fervor, with indignation. I listened to him and thought: should I cry or laugh? After the sentence, which was, however, quite lenient and conditional, I invited this scoundrel to my home for a chat. At first he looked at me suspiciously, then, realizing that there would probably be a drink, he went.

There was a drink, and we had a most curious conversation. I told the guy about the misfortunes of the unemployed during the NEP years, hoping to awaken in him gratitude for our extraordinary times, when it is not man who seeks work, but, on the contrary, work with many voices from all sides calls man to itself.

He looked at me with a contemptuous and indulgent smile: well, why are you going broke, why are you pestering me, we understand everything ourselves.

- So you were born under tsarism, that's what you were supposed to do - work like a donkey. But we were born under socialism, how can there be any comparison?

He finished his glass and walked away with a proud, independent air, this man "born under socialism." And I remembered the sorrowful words of the Samarkand dervish Kerim Abdallah: "Truly, descendants are never grateful to their ancestors for what was done for them, for all the losses and sacrifices suffered for their sake. They come to a house without asking who built it, they sit down at the table and forget to ask who grew the rice for this pilaf and who prepared the butter. I say, I do not complain, for I myself am such an ungrateful descendant and deservedly suffer from those who follow." This law, once universal, continues, unfortunately, to be partially in effect in our time. But a decree has finally been adopted on such fruits, "born under socialism" - it's high time!

However, I have strayed from the main subject of my story - the trading company "Tabachnikovs, father and son". This company perished before my eyes and under special circumstances, which should be told about.

Having lost my job at the shooting range, I was once again left without work. I went to the labor exchange and signed up for the waiting list under number four hundred and seventy-eight. "Is there any hope?" I asked the old woman who was in charge of the registration. She, gray, quiet, completely intimidated by the rude abuse and scandals of the unemployed, timidly, like a mouse, squeaked in response: "I don't know how to say it, but there are many of us who wait two years..." I realized that there was no hope.

I went to the road master's office, but there was a pre-winter layoff of track repair workers going on, and only a few were allowed to stay in the barracks for the winter as a special favor; the rest were thrown out into the street.

"Come in the spring, maybe I'll take you," said the master. "You're a healthy guy, you'll be good for hauling rails."

"Rails, so be it, that's not bad either," I thought, "but how and where am I supposed to live until spring?"

Chance came to my rescue, chance again, for the umpteenth time! Generally speaking, if you think about it, chance seems to the mind to be something very mysterious, as if having its own will: it invariably favors some people, while for others it is the opposite. It is good for Muslims who profess Islam - for them there is no chance, there is a predetermination of fate, but for us, who do not believe in predetermination, sometimes we have to anxiously reflect on the place and meaning of chance in our lives.

It was chance, in its purest form, that brought me together with Matvey Semenovich Tabachnikov, the head of the firm. I saw a cart loaded with mulberry logs on the street and followed it in the hope of cutting the logs into firewood, because the driver was old, weak and could not chop. I realized all this in a second: necessity is a good teacher. And if I had not followed the cart then, this story would not have happened - here is a chance for you! The cart stopped at some gate, I entered the yard, opened the gate, let the cart pass, helped the old man unload the logs, then called:

- Hey, master!

No one answered, but the windows in the house were open, which meant the owner was in the rooms. I went closer to the house and called louder, and a short, unshaven old man in a dressing gown, warm felt slippers and a quilted cotton cap appeared on the terrace covered with yellowed bindweed. He and the driver began a long argument over twenty kopecks, and finally the driver drove away, and the owner fixed me with a questioning look from his dull eyes with red eyelids, devoid of eyelashes. I said in a deliberately cheerful, confident voice, as if about a matter already decided:

- Let's chop! Where is your cleaver?

"What?" the owner asked again.

— Where is the cleaver, I ask?

"There, to the barn," he answered and left, dragging his thick, warm shoes along the ground.

I didn't notice that he didn't answer in Russian: "There, in the shed"; delighted with the unexpected earnings, I began to cut the logs. They turned out to be intertwined, difficult to cut, but I used wedges and managed to finish them by lunchtime. Then I stacked the chopped firewood by the fence in a beautiful, even woodpile, making cells on both sides. The wood of the mulberry is yellow, my woodpile was so cheerfully yellow with fresh chips under the transparent autumn sun.

I called the owner in a cheerful voice - it's ready! But he still looked gloomy and dull, chewed his lips and said:

— You should have put it in the shed, there, in the shed, I told you.

It turns out he wasn't mistaken, didn't misspeak in his answer, said exactly what he wanted to say. But I asked where the splitting axe was, not where to put the firewood! I darkened, frowned, but still took apart the woodpile, carried the firewood to the shed and stacked it again - of course, not as beautifully and evenly as the first time.

The owner gave me fifty kopecks.

- What? - I said, holding the coin in my palm. - Fifty kopecks for everything - for chopping, laying and re-laying!

"No," he replied. "I already have a janitor, but he went home to the village today."

Finally, I realized: my interlocutor was as deaf as an old mossy stump in the forest, and he understood all my words inside out.

"Not enough!" I yelled at the top of my lungs, pointing my finger at the coin. "Chop, pack, repack!"

This time he heard.

"Who ordered the chopping block from you?" he replied. "You were ordered to move it to the shed, that's all."

- Why did I inject? He shrugged.

- I don't know, maybe for my own pleasure, for gymnastics. A young man needs gymnastics.

Yes, I got a flinty old man, as hard to pay as his logs to cut up. And no wedges can be used here! I got angry, but I couldn't hold back my laughter. It's a great thing to be able to see the comic side of an unpleasant turn of events, how many times it has saved me! A person completely devoid of this ability is truly "nature's sad stepson"; in my life I have met many such ghouls.

- That's right! - I shouted to the old man with a laugh. - I really did chop your wood for my own pleasure, for the sake of gymnastics, you don't have to pay me. Thank you!

I bowed exaggeratedly. A strange gleam flashed in his teary eyes, and he replied:

- You're a cheerful and not angry guy, I like people like that. Digging in his pocket with his bony fingers, he pulled out a second fifty-kopeck piece and handed it to me, explaining:

— To complete the pleasure, vodka before dinner.

- I don't drink vodka.

- You don't drink? That's a rarity these days. If you really don't drink, I can invite you to have dinner with me.

I was very surprised, embarrassed, began to politely refuse, but it is very difficult to be polite and shout at the same time, I spoke quietly, he did not hear and headed for the terrace, thinking that I had accepted his invitation to dinner. What else could I do - not show him my back contrary to all the rules of politeness? I followed him.

It was a strange house - spacious, rich, but seemingly uninhabited. All the furniture was covered with sheets, the pictures on the walls were hung with thick paper, yellowed by the sun and spotted by flies, the bronze was covered with dust, the porcelain in the expensive antique cabinet was under a key, the piano was covered with a blanket with red fringe. The old man left me to wait, went away and appeared only twenty minutes later, completely transformed, shaved, dressed, with false teeth.

We dined together, a moustached, sullen old woman served, looking at me very disapprovingly - under her gaze, the food would not go down my throat. But the host was friendly, courteous, and I dined well. The only annoying thing was the host's excessive curiosity - where I was from, who and how did I end up in Andizhan. I had to tear myself away from my plate all the time, because it is impolite to talk with a full mouth.

- So, your father sent you from home...

- Yes, father.

- A smart man. He sent you to find out how much a pound of trouble sells for in the world. And what did you find out?

138

- Not really yet.

— You'll find out later.

For some reason the old man switched to the informal "you" with me. Dinner was already over, the old woman was collecting the plates. I said, trying to express myself elegantly:

— I still don't know your first and middle names, so I'm forced to thank you anonymously.

"Matvey Semenovich Tabachnikov," he introduced himself and handed me a form on which was printed in beautiful English font at the top: "Trading firm Tabachnikovs, father and son. Odessa, Kanatnaya, 18, own house, telephone 53–82." There was a hard sign; the form was pre-revolutionary.

"I understand," I said, "before the revolution you had your own business in Odessa."

"We still have a business, we run a haberdashery store," the old man answered with dignity.

I realized: I entered this spacious house through the gate, from behind, and its façade faces Sovetskaya, the center of all Andijan's shops and stalls.

"So you are the Triumph of Grace!" I exclaimed.

"Yes," the old man answered smugly. "We have the best haberdashery, the very best. We get our goods from Leningrad, not from Moscow. Leningrad and Moscow are two very different places in elegance, let me tell you. And before, in Odessa, we sold only Parisian goods. Once, Prince Oldenburgsky, His Imperial Highness, from the august family, came to see us in Odessa. He bought two handkerchiefs. And even earlier, the famous film actress Vera Kholodnaya came to see us. I offered her Lyon lace for underwear. "Who will be the lucky one you deign to contemplate this lace?" I said. She laughed. "The lace is rare, but too expensive even for me." "Oh!" I exclaimed. "That's nothing. You'll have a thirty percent discount, just give me your signed photograph." She gave me a signed photograph, took the lace and left. And I gave this card and a sample of Lyon lace to the "Odessky Listok", and an advertisement appeared there: "Vera Kholodnaya bought Lyon lace for pantaloons from us." And at the bottom, in large, half-inch letters: "Young people, attention!" What do you think? The next day, all the Odessa ladies bought Lyon lace from us! Commerce is an art, young man! And do you know commercial correspondence?

With this question the old man immediately revealed everything to me. Permanent service, that's what he was getting at. Permanent service is the ultimate dream of every unemployed man! But I didn't know commercial correspondence. It was scary to admit it, so I answered evasively:

- A little... I have a general idea.

- It's nothing, you'll learn, - said the old man. - I have a book with samples of commercial correspondence. You just have to replace the words: instead of "dear sir" write "dear citizen". And what's your handwriting like?

"Average, fairly legible," I replied, although in fact my handwriting was ugly and confused. "I also type a little."

- Oh! - said the old man. - In Odessa we had a typewriter from the American company "Smith-Premier". What a typewriter!

"Underwood is better," I remarked casually.

— You think? But "Smis-premier" has two fonts - large and small, both separately.

- It's already outdated. On Underwood, the fonts are unified.

- Mmm... - The old man chewed his lips discontentedly. - Not everything that is new is better, personally I prefer "Smith-Premier"... Well, now you have guessed, I hope?

Thank God he didn't make me write in his presence. And then I'll try to develop my handwriting.

"Have you guessed?" the old man repeated.

— You, I think, want to entrust me with the management of commercial correspondence.

"Yes," said the old man. "Why else would I invite you to dinner? Old Tabachnikov does nothing without payment. You see, we run the business together, my son and I. My son is temporarily absent at the moment, and I need an honest, modest assistant. Salary – thirty rubles a month, without any additional payments to the union or the health insurance fund. To outsiders, you are my nephew. Do you agree?"

Of course! That same day I moved into the haberdashery, into the back room where the boxes of goods were kept, laid out my bed on the cot, immensely grateful to the old man for free lodging on top of his salary. But old Tabachnikov did nothing without calculation - in me he acquired both an assistant and a night watchman, which he himself explained to me in response to my grateful outpourings.

However, at night little was required of me - to leave the door leading to the store open, nothing more.

But there was plenty of work during the day. The old man entrusted the haberdashery shop to me in its entirety: I kept records, kept correspondence, gave the clerk the goods, received the boxes that arrived from Leningrad on the railway, and on Thursdays I took the balances and entered them into a special register. The clerk was a red-haired, freckled man, always sad about something, with a long, sad nose and the same sad, drawn-out voice; he would offer a customer, say, buttons, but it seemed as if he were offering a funeral wreath. It was impossible to imagine a worse clerk for a haberdashery shop. But still, trade was brisk, and the old man made three hundred net profits every week. In addition, he would disappear for days on end on other business, also, one must assume, not unprofitable, but I was not privy to these matters. The old man would briefly explain that he was going about Stein's business, and that was all.

In those years, on many magazine covers one could read the following announcement: "The latest Paris fashion, a necklace of artificial pearls, French "Conta" type, 42 cm — 11 sizes 40 kopecks, 49 cm — 14 sizes 40 kopecks and 130 cm — 26 sizes 40 kopecks (all with silver clasps). L. Stein, Leningrad, Nakhimson Avenue, 29)3." So, Matvey Semenovich Tabachnikov was L. Stein's representative in Andijan, and there was only one thing that was surprising: why did this representation take up so much of Matvey Semenovich's time, as if he had set himself the imperative and sacred goal of decorating all Andijan women, including Uzbek women, with pearl necklaces of the French "Conta" type?

Once I expressed my thoughts about this representation to the clerk. The clerk smiled, but did not answer.

Later, when we got used to each other, he became more talkative. It is known that all servants in the world are always inclined to talk about their masters in a condemning way, and we were Matvey Semyonovich's servants, and we also wanted to talk in a condemning way... So day after day, word after word - and the old man began to appear before me in a different light.

At that time, a new type of negotiation was being established in the country (but did not have time to establish itself), not the classic English or Dutch type, but a mixed Russian-American, or more precisely, Odessa-Yaroslavl-American. From tsarist Odessa, it inherited the combination skills and inclinations for swindles, from old Yaroslavl - resourcefulness and shrewd swindling, from Americanism it borrowed merciless, purposeful predation. This negotiation, in order to beat the purely American one in all respects, lacked only the scale, which was in every way limited by the tireless vigilance of the financial departments and investigative bodies.

Activists of this type - they were called "Nepmen" in the American manner - were always balancing on the finest edge, where commerce subtly and delicately, quite imperceptibly, crossed over into criminality. I mean concealing income in order to avoid paying taxes. They were not arrested for this, because all Nepmen would have to be arrested without exception - they limited themselves to fines. But there were more serious acts: smuggling, currency and gold transactions, drug trafficking, buying stolen goods, selling counterfeit chervonets, and running underground gambling houses. For this, they were imprisoned under the relevant articles of the Criminal Code.

As I understood from the clerk's hints, Matvey Semenovich Tabachnikov took either direct part, or more often indirect complicity, in most of the above-mentioned acts, hiding behind his tireless concerns about the prosperity of L. Stein's firm. He didn't get caught for a long time, he walked free, but in the end he was caught for something. At the time when I was chopping wood for him, having lunch with him and then working in his store, he was serving a two-year prison sentence.

There is no typo here, wait, it didn't become clear to me right away either. The clerk kept this main secret of the owner from me, I got to the bottom of it myself.

Friday was a holiday in Central Asia, on Thursdays the shop closed at three o'clock, and I took the leftovers. That Thursday, having locked the door behind the clerk, I began my usual business, and suddenly the owner came, wanting to take the leftovers himself, to check. Well, we got down to business together. But half an hour later the front door began to hum and shake under someone's mighty fist. I opened it and saw a short, curly-haired fellow with thick, brazenly turned-out lips.

"What do you want?" I asked unfriendly. "Can't you see, the store is closed?"

"Get out of the way, you bastard!" he replied in a bass voice and, pushing me aside, stepped into the store and approached Matvey Semenovich.

The old man was embarrassed, I realized that my presence here was unnecessary, he went to his room, closing the door tightly behind him.

But the door was thin, and the owner of the bass, apparently knowing about the old man's deafness, spoke in a raised voice, and I heard everything against my will.

"What do I care about your five chervonets?" boomed the bass. "There's no use in the Naples cabaret with five chervonets. Give me fifteen, and not a kopeck less."

In response, the old man's muttering was indistinct, quiet, but excited. The bass objected:

- I knock together fifteen boxes every day and ten on Thursdays, eighty-five boxes a week. So, all this for five chervonets? Besides, I haven't come the last two Thursdays and haven't received any money from you.

- You broke something and they took it away from you, it's your own fault! - the old man squealed. - Take six chervonets and get out...

"Where to?" the bass answered menacingly. "Maybe there..."

- Blackmailer! - The old man groaned dully and began to wail in a language not in Russian.

"Okay then," concluded the bass. "Twelve chervonets, so as not to quarrel."

He apparently received twelve chervonets, the front door slammed shut, and there was silence. I waited a bit and opened my door. The old man, pale, was alone in the store, clutching his heart, on the counter lay haberdashery that we had not yet checked - boxes of buttons, threads, rolls of braid and lace.

"Shall we continue?" I asked. He waved his hand weakly and walked away, leaving me alone. As I removed the remains and wrote them down in the book, I thought about the strange visitor, about the verbal altercation behind the door - all of this gave off a distinct smell of criminality.

Winter had not yet arrived, the sky was still blue and the sun was shining, only in the mornings it was slightly frosty, and the breeze was sharp, fragrant, wintery.

In my free time I would rent a bicycle and ride out of town, into the fields and gardens, already leafless, transparently and sadly showing through with a thin lace of branches. There is a difference for the eye between spring, still leafless gardens and autumn, already leafless ones, perhaps because in spring, under the warm winds, the bare branches wave, sway, live, but in autumn they are motionless in a sunny pre-winter numbness.

About seven miles from the city stood a three-mill water mill on a large deep ditch, owned by a certain Babajan. The owner, tall, bearded, white from flour dust, greeted me warmly, baked an unleavened flatbread from warm flour on a hot stone, straight from the millstone, and treated me to tea. He kept trying to ride his bicycle, but fell down as soon as I let go of the bicycle. "Shaitan is a donkey!" he shouted, smearing laughing tears across his face. "Only devils can ride it!"

The water was rustling under the mill, the millstones were moving merrily, smoothly, with a hum, and under the roof the turtledoves, which lived here in great numbers, were scurrying about with the silky rustle of their wings.

Once I asked Babajan if the mill was making much money. Friendship gave me the right to ask such a question.

"It gives a good profit," Babajan answered, "but the owner takes half of it."

— Isn't the mill yours?

— Where would I get the money to buy a mill like that with three mills? I rent it on a share basis from a man in the city. He rents out five more mills in the area, mine is the sixth. True, I rent it without a paper, but we agreed in front of the mullah.

This was a very common method of concealing income in Central Asia at that time - instead of a written agreement subject to accounting by the financial department, a verbal agreement was concluded in front of the mullah, and the financial department was left out. I was not surprised by this, I was shocked to hear from Babajan the name of the real owner of the mill - Tabachnikov.

- Matvey Semenovich! - I exclaimed.

I was returning from the mill in the evening, the gardens were sad in the quiet half-light of the autumn dawn, the muezzin was singing on the distant minaret, and his prayerful call was heard for a long time along the way. I forgot about Matvey Semenovich, but when I returned the bike to the workshop, the owner said to me:

— Sign up for an installment plan. English bicycles from the BAS company, brand "Three Guns", new, sealed, sold with a guarantee and in installments for six months. Only six pieces, I said that about fifteen should be written out, but Matvey Semenovich wrote out only six.

- Why Matvey Semenovich and not you?

- But he is the owner, and I am just for show.

Here in the city, bicycle workshops, there in the villages, mills! And everywhere there were front men, to divert attention! The old man's truly greedy hands reached further than one might think. I was finally convinced that the haberdashery shop "Triumph of Elegance" and the representative office of the L. Stein firm were all just a disguise, a cover, and that the old man did his real business underground. And maybe the Matilda confectionery opposite, where the flirtatious pretty waitress Zhenya serves such fragrant, delicious chocolate, also actually belongs to the old man, and not at all to the plump, blonde Madame Stivinskaya, who poses as the owner, and the buffet of the goggle-eyed fat Dzhokhadze in the city garden is in fact the buffet of Matvey Semenovich, and the cabaret "Naples" is also his, and in general he, the new Marquis of Karabas, invisibly owns all the city trade... The world began to ghostly double in my eyes - behind every face of any kvass seller, any shashlik maker, I seemed to see Matvey Semenovich, his red, watery eyelids, his sunken, toothless mouth with thin, gray, eternally chewing lips... But this is still a trifle - ordinary trade, you can profit from this only by concealing income. I was sure that the old man was involved in other secret affairs and was possibly involved in the recent robbery of the savings bank in the old town. Who was that burly fellow who came to him last Thursday and why didn't the old man dare refuse the fellow money, but gave him twelve ducats for a drink? Eh?.. It was worth thinking about, there was a whiff of Conan Doyle here, the old man, recreated by my imagination, turned into a mysterious, sinister figure.

Meanwhile, a week flew by, and on another Thursday, after the trade had closed, the old man came to the store again - he still wanted to personally remove and check the remains. And again, in the midst of our work, the door hummed under the mighty blows of a fist: a curly-haired young man with turned-out lips appeared.

I don't know how many chervonets the old man gave him this time, but when the young man left triumphantly and I left my room for the store, the old man said in a weak, fading voice:

- If I give like this every week, what will be left for me?

"Well, let's say there will be some left for you, there really will be some left," I thought.

I had to finish the work of removing the remains alone again.

The days after the holidays - Saturday and Sunday - were considered rich days in our shop. There were plenty of buyers, or rather buyers, because the stronger sex showed complete indifference to the products of the haberdashery industry, as well as to the products of the confectionery art of Madame Stivinskaia, on the contrary, preferring to everything in the world the buffet of the goggle-eyed Dzhokhadze in the city garden: there, under the guise of tea, they served colored moonshine in teapots, and by midday, dashing songs were heard from the garden next to the buffet.

Madame Bobrova, the wife of the local sausage maker, and citizen Stozharova, the wife of the head of the agricultural department, had just left the shop. After them, the shop had acquired a smashed appearance, many cartons were piled up in disarray on the counter - the ladies had been choosing, but had left without choosing anything, having decided to smash another, competing shop, Agriropoulos. By the way, to test a person's endurance, it is best to put him behind the counter of a ladies' shop for a day - ladies spend their money wisely, not everyone could endure it and was valued by the owner for this. Putting away the cartons, tidying up the shelves, absentmindedly listening to a drunken song coming to us from the city garden, the clerk said:

- Dzhokhadze rented a second buffet at the station and yesterday invited me to work as a buffet attendant. I refused.

- Why?

- I'm afraid of drunks, I don't know how to deal with them.

"What about the drunks?" I said dismissively. "You can easily deal with a drunk: trip him up and he's done for, down. But dealing with bandits and robbers - that's more serious."

— With what bandits?

— With those who robbed the savings bank in the old town.

— Where could you see them?

- Here, in the store.

And I told him about the double appearance of a burly young man with his lips turned out.

- He looks like he just escaped from prison yesterday. He's a clear bandit.

The clerk looked at me with a strange look.

- This is Boris Matveyevich, the owner's son! He really does come home from prison on leave on Thursdays, but he's not a bandit at all.

Son! I remembered: the old man told me something about his son, about his temporary absence.

"Why did he go to prison?" I asked.

— It wasn't he who got into jail, Matvey Semenovich did, and he's just sitting it out.

At first I understood the shop assistant's words figuratively: the old man had done something, and his son had taken the blame. It turned out that it was not so, the shop assistant's words should have been understood in the direct, most literal sense. Matvey Semenovich himself was tried at the end of spring, a sentence of two years was passed on Matvey Semenovich himself, and he himself was sent to prison. The son remained on the sidelines, and did not even testify in the case. But then the events took a completely fantastic turn.

After two months of imprisonment, the old man was allowed a weekly daily leave home from Thursday to Friday for exemplary behavior in prison. In those years, it seemed that the indisputability and righteousness of the socialist principles of life had already been understood and accepted by everyone, and people who violated the new fair laws did so as if out of an old habit, contrary to their consciousness, so the course was aimed at re-education, at the conscious elimination of old habits, and from this, liberalism was inevitably born, like the aforementioned vacations from prison. In those years, the communists lived far ahead of the slow times, as, incidentally, they live now, and in this rapid flight, of course, mistakes were made when the communists attributed their inherent winged spirit to all people.

The method of persuasion was also applied to Matvey Semenovich in prison. But the old man was not one of those who could be reforged, the old man was made of flint and belonged entirely, with all his guts, to the old world that had gone into oblivion. Sitting in his cell, knocking together wooden boxes - fifteen boxes daily, his soul and mind were constantly occupied with his acquisitive scams, machinations and combinations that remained behind the prison walls.

During those first two months, when the old man was sitting without vacations, the junior partner, his son Boris Matveyevich, was in charge of the firm's affairs. Father and son had opposite personalities: the father was a money-grubber, a hoarder, and the son was a spendthrift, a carouser. Previously, his father had not given him much scope, but with the old man's departure to prison, the chains fell apart, and the son began to spin, go wild, and go on a spree at the Naples cabaret in the company of cheerful girls. When visiting the old man in prison, he, of course, said nothing about his carousing and presented the old man's affairs to the firm in the most rosy colors. All the louder was the scandal that erupted one Thursday when the old man, quite unexpectedly for his son, appeared before him.

The old man found the company's affairs in complete disarray: the goods that had arrived from Leningrad lay unclaimed in the railway warehouse, and penalties for storage had already accumulated on them to an extent that absorbed all the expected profits; some bills had not been paid, others had not been received - in a word, everything was rapidly going downhill.

The old man spent the whole of Friday untangling the cases, and at seven o'clock, the time to return to prison, he said to his son:

- You, tramp from Moldovanka, if you can't be entrusted with the affairs of the company, then you can be entrusted with serving time - go to prison for me! At the roll call, when they call Tabachnikov, you will shout back: "Here!" - that's all.

I don't know the prison regime of those times, but apparently the regime wasn't very strict, the old man's clever scheme worked, and none of the bosses noticed that the old Tabachnikov was replaced at inspections by the young Tabachnikov. And the old man quickly straightened things out and strengthened the firm, which had been completely shaken. But the old man left his son, as a prison inheritance, in addition to the unfortunate duty of nailing together fifteen wooden boxes every day, his weekly vacations, and on Thursdays after dinner the son would come under his father's roof. He would come home from prison angry, gloomy, and in a harsh tone, which is only spoken by indisputable right, demanding money for the Naples cabaret; at first he was content with five chervonets, then he raised this figure to seven, and now even ten chervonets was not enough for him: cheerful girls are not cheap company.

I heard these family quarrels, sitting in my room at the store, behind a thin door. Both times the son won, and the old man remained defeated. And the third dispute ended in death for the old man.

I heard a third dispute. This time the son, who had just come from prison, demanded a mind-boggling sum - twenty chervonets. He cited some billiard debt of his.

- It's a debt of honor, daddy! - he boomed behind the door. - Our family name is threatened with shame. Read Leo Tolstoy's novel "War and Peace", where Count Nikolai Rostov loses thirty thousand of the Tsar's gold Nikolaev money at cards, and his father, the old count, meekly pays the debt for his son. He doesn't want his son, the young count, to get his face beaten up, so he pays. His son's face is more valuable to him than money, he's a real father! And you don't care if I get my face beaten up. Be ashamed, daddy!

- Let the Count pay if he likes! - the old man shouted back in a shrill voice. - The serfs worked for the Count, the Count had a lot of extra money, but I don't have any! Listen, tramp, I will not pay any debts for you!

"You won't?" the son asked ominously.

"I won't!" the old man squealed.

They left the shop together, arguing as they went. I locked the door behind them. I was troubled by a vague premonition of trouble; if I had been the owner, I would have given my son twenty chervonets, his tone was very decisive today.

On Friday we did not trade, I spent the whole day in the old city at the bazaar. Late autumn bazaars were especially rich and crowded in Central Asia: having gathered in the harvest, the villagers came to the city, sold the fruits of their labor and had fun in the teahouses to the sounds of dutars[14] and tambourines. And the sky was already gloomy, occasionally a thin rain fell, the wind, rustling on robes and turbans, blew more and more gusty, carrying cold dry dust.

On Saturday, after lunch, the younger co-owner of the trading company, the son, showed up at the store. The clerk and I exchanged glances: he should have been in prison, not in the store.

"How's business?" he inquired, sticking out his thick lower lip. "How much is in the till?"

---

[14] Dutar is a plucked string instrument with a large pear-shaped body and a long neck.

"Ninety-two rubles and some kopecks," the clerk answered after a pause.

- Let's!

- And what will Matvey Semenovich say?

"Come on, they say!" the junior partner roared, opened the cash register, took the proceeds, went into my room, counted the boxes of goods and left.

"Interesting!" I said as the door closed behind him.

"Nothing interesting," the clerk replied. "He just promised to give it to someone in prison, so they gave him a two-day vacation."

- But where did he put the old man?

Hearing my question, the clerk turned pale. Looking at him, I turned pale too. We both thought of a terrible murder.

"We must report him before he manages to escape," said the clerk. "Stay in the store, and I'll go to the police."

While he was walking, a cab pulled up to the store, in the carriage sat Boris Matveyevich and Agriropoulo, the owner of a competing trading firm, a thin, sharp-nosed Greek with black bird-like eyes, very close together. The young owner led the competitor into my room, where the boxes with the goods were kept, and bargaining began between them.

The owner was selling the entire warehouse at the store at once, wholesale. He was in a hurry, he needed money, immediately, right now, and the cunning Greek took advantage of this, opened the boxes, found some flaws in the goods, shook his bird-like head and clicked his tongue. I grew cold, hearing how the young owner was selling the boxes to him for half price. The clerk returned, I whispered to him:

— Selling a warehouse.

- Let it be so!

The clerk waved his hand hopelessly.

- And the old man?

- The old man is no more. That is, he is alive, he is sitting in prison. Yesterday the son sent his dad to prison and now he is the complete master.

Sent daddy to prison! There was something ugly, unnatural, unbearably disgusting about it; I went out into the street so as not to hear the greedy, impatient bass of the owner and the chattering tenor of Agriropoulo. Then I ran after three carts, loaded the boxes, the carts left, the owner left with pockets full of chervonets, the clerk and I were left alone in the store, the clerk said:

"I'll have to go to Dzhokhadze as a barman; in a week there won't be anything to do here."

There were another twenty boxes in the warehouse on the railroad, the owner and I got them and took them straight to the competitor's store, or rather, a former competitor, because now he has become a monopolist in haberdashery in Andijan.

And our shop was wasting away and dying out with each passing day, while the Naples cabaret was shining with lights until four in the morning, and the sounds of a Romanian orchestra, the clatter of billiard balls, drunken shouts, and women's squeals could be heard from there—young Tabachnikov was wasting his life there in the company of cheerful girls, and the prison wall was darkening heavily and silently, illuminated only in four places, above the watchtowers in the corners, and in a locked cell sat an old man, deprived of leave for his cunning scam of sending his son to prison instead of himself, and I was restlessly tossing and turning on my bed in the empty warehouse, wondering where I should go now, and outside the persistent autumn rain was gurgling, hurriedly whispering, and vaguely babbling, blowing up bubbles in the yellow puddles.

The clerk went to Dzhokhadze as a barman, and I was left alone in the store. There was nothing to sell, the shelves were empty, and I spent whole days reading Dickens. The young owner, having destroyed the store to the ground, never came back, being busy ruining all the other enterprises of the firm. I heard rumors that he was selling off the bills of exchange left by the old man ahead of schedule for half price, and was selling something else, also for half price. From the miller Babajan I learned that the mills, all six of them, had also passed into other hands. The firm was burning with a hot flame, and the cabaret "Naples" was flourishing as never before - now the young owner had finally moved to "Naples" and often spent the night there in a separate office.

Soon he began to think about selling the house together with the shop. Buyers came, looked at the house, the shop; the barman Dzhokhadze came too – the most respectable buyer. Dzhokhadze was in no hurry, but the young owner was in a hurry and day by day he lowered the price: as always, he needed the money immediately, right now. Finally the deal was done, Dzhokhadze warned me that in a week he would open his third – winter – bar in the shop. Two carpenters appeared, began to build a bar counter, and in my room an elderly stove-maker was laying down a stove for cooking hot dishes – I lived among resinous shavings, scattered bricks, among buckets of lime mortar and clay.

Dzhokhadze offered me to work as a waiter in his buffet, but the former store clerk, who had now joined Dzhokhadze, advised me against it. "You won't be able to," he said. "After all, you won't be putting empty beer bottles under the table for drunks, and you can't do without that, that's what all trade depends on."

A month and a half had passed since the old man had been firmly in prison; one Thursday, a prisoner, on leave from prison, came into the shop, which had almost completely been converted into a buffet, and asked for the young owner.

"He's not here," I replied. "What should I tell him?"

- Tell him that your father is very upset - for a month and a half, his son has not come to see him even once.

In the evening I went to the cabaret "Naples" and found the young owner in the billiard room. Without a jacket, stretched out on the green baize, with his leg raised high, he was fidgeting with the cue in the chalked hollow between his thumb and forefinger, carefully aiming at the ball hanging over the corner pocket. He was very swollen since the day I last saw him, from drunkenness and sleepless nights, I suppose; some two people with dissolute, haggard faces were fussing, hovering, fawning around him.

"Boris Matveyevich," I began, at that moment he hit, and the ball didn't hit the pocket, but went for a walk and circled around the table, bouncing off the elastic sides.

- Arm in arm! - Boris Matveevich yelled, rushing towards me and waving his cue. - What the hell do you want here?

- The old man, your father, is very offended by you, you never came to prison to visit him.

- What business is it of yours? - he yelled. - He came to yap under my arm? Throw him out of here, throw him out!..

Two hangers-on jumped up to me, but I grabbed a heavy bone ball from the table and they stopped.

"Scoundrel!" I said to Boris Matveyevich's face.

- Give me the ball, the ball! - the marker yelled and rushed after me up the stairs. I gave him the ball and went down to the exit of the cabaret.

In the restaurant, the Romanian orchestra was already playing its sweet, sensitive melodies with the dying trembling of the violins; at the cloakroom, cheerful Andizhan girls were undressing and preening in front of the mirror—Boris Matveyevich's constant company.

The feud between the Tabachnikovs, father and son, did not really concern me, especially since I no longer worked for their firm; whoever was in prison, father or son, they deserved it, and the right thing to do would have been to put them both away at once. But you can feel sorry for any punished criminal, unless he is a murderer, so I went to the prison with a bundle of various food in my hands, to see the old man.

- You? - the old man said in surprise. - Why not Boris?

In those years, I was too young to sugarcoat the bitter truth, so I told the old man everything about my son and the company. He listened and his spirits sank, as if the air was leaving him, like rubber. He, of course, expected to hear something bad, prepared himself for it, but my news killed him.

"And the store?" he asked again.

"And the store," I confirmed.

— And the mills?

— And the mills...

— And bills of exchange?

- And bills of exchange...

He was silent for a long time, looking at the barred, dust-clouded window. In the corner, on a stool, sat the warden, dozing, leaning against the wall.

"It was to be expected," said the old man in a wooden, emotionless voice. "That's all he knows how to do - ruin businesses and throw away money."

"Ten minutes left," the warden warned from the corner and dozed off again.

"Listen," the old man said in a half-whisper, "he's ruining the business, but he doesn't know everything. I still have capital in other cities. He hasn't gotten there yet, but he can.

- He will definitely get there...

- Yes! - the old man squealed, but, coming to his senses, he again switched to a half-whisper. - Listen, let's speak frankly, you are an honest and efficient guy, I believe you. You will be my partner, for now I will allocate you a quarter of the capital, and when I die, the business will pass to you entirely. Do you want it?

"That's impossible," I said. "But you have a son…"

"He's a dog to me, worse than a dog!" the old man whispered. "I renounce him. He's ruining the business, and I renounce him... He must be removed."

I did not immediately understand the ominous meaning of these words. The old man continued:

- You will go to Margelan, I will give you the address. There you will get a thousand, even one and a half thousand, I will write from prison. Five hundred - for you.

"For what?" I exclaimed.

"Five hundred for you," the old man repeated. "And for a thousand you'll talk someone into removing it… Or removing it yourself. Completely removing it… And no one will ever know, never!"

I understood the old man and looked at him with amazement and fear, and he had gone completely mad. His lips were twitching, his hands were shaking, tears were running down his cheeks, he was no longer whispering, but moaning.

— …It's ruining the business… We need to get rid of it… You'll be the junior partner…

I took him by the shoulders and shook him.

- Come to your senses, Matvey Semenovich. After all, he is your son. And how could you think that I would commit murder? What do I care about your company, about your family accounts?

"Understand, understand, he's ruining us!" the old man muttered in a feverish half-whisper, grabbed my hands, stretched out his sinewy neck, and brought his tear-stained face closer to me. "Another two months, and there will be nothing left, nothing..."

"The meeting is over," the warden announced. "Tabachnikov, to the cell!"

As he was leaving, the old man turned to me conspiratorially and hit me across the throat with the edge of his hand.

The city of Andizhan seemed strange to me when, having left the prison, I went out onto the main street. It was raining, gurgling, whispering, babbling, blowing bubbles in the muddy puddles; it was getting dark; the cabaret, casino, restaurants, circus, cinemas lit their inviting lights; music was coming from everywhere - Romanian melodies, waltzes, hopak and lezginka, all mixed up. And under every sign, in every entrance, I seemed to see a murder, already committed or impending, from everywhere the face of old Tabachnikov floated towards me, distorted by malicious madness, flooded with tears of impotent rage. I also remembered his son, stretched out on a billiard table with a cue in his hands and his leg raised high, and he too smelled thickly and suffocatingly of crime... Thus the seamy side of the old world, its remnants, feasting on the main street of Andijan or sitting in prison, was laid bare before me. At that time, all this was only vague feelings, but later, having settled, they rose to consciousness and gave birth in me to a great hatred for any acquisitiveness, for any unrighteous property received from the devil at the cost of one's own living soul...

I spent the next night in Andijan in a teahouse located quite far from the main street. I had money.

I paid the teahouse owner, Kurban Niyaz, for several blankets, which he spread out for me on the flat roof of the teahouse, and I stretched out on them with pleasure, experiencing a feeling of healthy languor and complete peace of mind.

The rain had stopped, and an ashen night haze hung around. The stars were clear, close and transparent, as if they were shining through from within.

I didn't feel like sleeping, and I began to make plans for my future life, or rather, to think about a new service that would give me a livelihood.

What can you do if that's how it really was? In those years, the clumsy words "finding a living" had the most direct and full-fledged meaning, lost now, when no one "finds a living" any more, but, on the contrary, finds work to their taste, to their liking. Of course, we could not even imagine such luxury!.. Meanwhile, I do not regret at all that my youth was difficult and sometimes in semi-starvation: driven by the need to "find", I visited many places, met many people, gained life experience, hardened myself against all sorts of adversity and thus safely avoided the shameful years of adult foolishness.

In the morning I counted my money, there was very little of it after paying Niyaz for a pot of tea and a flatbread.

There was no point in thinking about leaving Andijan; I had to find a new job right away. Niyaz, apparently, guessed about my thoughts and advised me to go to the Andijan court, where there was a vacancy for a journalist - not the one who writes for newspapers, but another journalist who records incoming and outgoing papers in an office journal. I thanked the teahouse owner and went to the court. I was lucky: I got the position and the title.

And I dreamed of becoming a real newspaper journalist!..

Once in the court corridor I saw a young woman. She was walking quickly towards me, reading some paper as she went; she had her hair combed smoothly, dressed very modestly in a blue women's suit with a skirt below the knees, unlike the Andijan fashionistas who wore skirts above the knees; she absentmindedly glanced at me, and I remembered her dark, beautiful eyes, her delicate face with thinly and

156

tenderly outlined lips, some special purity and clarity of her high forehead, which I just wanted to call a brow.

"Who is this beautiful Uzbek woman?" I asked one of the judge's clerks.

He grinned and shrugged.

- Judge Khalifa Tashmukhamedova. Sent from Tashkent. What times - women are appointed judges!..

And a week and a half later, I was present at a court hearing that Khalifa chaired.

It was a cheerful trial - the judges smiled reservedly, Khalifa smiled, the audience laughed openly, only the defendant did not laugh and hoarsely answered the court in a sullen, alienated voice.

The defendant is old man Smyslov, the most famous wild boar hunter in Andijan.

For melon fields and dzhugar[15] crops, the boar is the most devastating animal. It roams in herds, eats melons at will, only the ripest and sweetest. By the time it gets to the ripe one, to its taste, how many unripe ones it will rip apart with its tusks! An hour later, there is no melon field, everything is ruined, trampled... And the boar herd cuts the tall two-meter dzhugar clean, using its tusks like scissors...

At night, in the fields around Uzbek villages, watchmen climbed up on towers, lit fires and furiously beat bowls and buckets with mallets to scare away the wild boars. It helped, but not very well. That is why in any Uzbek village they would greet a city hunter with a double-barreled shotgun over his shoulder so warmly. Smyslov and his three sons would go hunting in two carts with a pack of dogs. The old man had been hunting wild boars for a long time, back in the tsarist times, and had acquired a large house.

He himself resembled a seasoned, grey-haired boar, squat, stooped, with a large head growing straight out of his shoulders, with a stiff stubble on his red, puffy face, and small, dull eyes. The latter, that is, the puffiness of his face and the dull, senseless look, resulted from the unrestrained drunkenness to which the old man indulged in between hunts. They said he could drink a quarter of the strongest moonshine in one sitting; I myself was not an eyewitness to such exploits of his, but I think it is true. But on the other hand, when hunting, he never took a single drop. "A boar is a serious, ferocious beast," he said, "it will dispose of a drunk man in an instant!" He

---

[15] *Djugara* (white durra) is a cereal of the sorghum genus, a grain and forage plant.

knew the boar's temperament – the old man's left leg did not bend, and he dragged it: a memory of an encounter with a twelve-pound cleaver.

From 1917 to 1922, no one hunted in Kokand: hunters were afraid of the Basmachi and did not go outside the city. Birds and animals bred freely, especially wild boars.

In 1922, when the Basmachi movement ended and it became safe to leave the city, the old man returned to his trade. In a short time, he built a second house for his eldest son. He was planning to build a third. Nothing surprising - the Smyslovs brought five, six, seven boar carcasses from hunting and handed them over to Vyaznikov's sausage shop, with whom the old man had an agreement. And in addition to money from Vyaznikov, he also received a bonus from the state - five rubles for each killed boar.

The old man got burned by these bonuses. And how could he not be tempted? The bonuses were paid by the district executive committee according to the number of boar tails. The old man came to the district executive committee with tails wrapped in newspaper. In front of the secretary and the policeman, he stood at a distance and counted the tails. Why at a distance? Because a boar, according to Muslim law, is a vile, unclean creature, "haram", even contemplating a boar is sinful for a Muslim, not to mention touching it.

A report was drawn up, the old man received the money, and then, in the presence of the secretary and the policeman, he either burned the tails or buried them in the ground.

One day he brought twenty-two tails. The secretary agreed to give a bonus only for fifteen. The old man took the remaining seven to the neighboring district and handed them in quite successfully in the same manner... On the way back, a commercial idea struck him: after all, tails can be sewn from the boar's skin on the back of the neck!

Planned - done. Now the Smyslov family went hunting, armed not only with guns, but also with needles. They sewed tails, wrapping a willow branch with boar bristles. Things went well - after all, the old man handed in the tails, as before, standing at a distance. True, now he had to go around several district executive committees, but what a disaster!..

But the old man, overcome by greed, became arrogant, impudent and was caught red-handed. He was sentenced to a fine and a suspended six-month prison sentence.

Such a light punishment surprised everyone, but the court chairperson, Khalifa Tashmukhamedova, explained that part of the blame should be placed on the secretary and the policeman, who, due to religious prejudices, did their job poorly and overlooked the deception.

Old man Smyslov was my first mentor in hunting in Andijan, that's why I'm talking about him in such detail. After the trial, he retired from the boar trade, handing it over to his sons, and he opened a gunsmith's shop in a shed at home.

Since the trial, he had great respect for the Khalifa and always said: "She is a woman and an Uzbek, but she has some intelligence in her head."

A few days after the trial of Smyslov, while wandering through the bazaar, I unexpectedly found myself witnessing a fight between Khalifa and the Andijan satrap Saakov.

At that time, commandant's offices still existed in the Central Asian cities - an echo of the civil war. The Basmachi had long since been routed, the scattered remnants of the Basmachi gangs wandered somewhere in the mountains, not daring to show themselves in the valley, passes and curfews had long since been abolished, but the commandant's offices still existed, although they had absolutely nothing to do - the police kept order, the Cheka suppressed the counterrevolution. The commandants languished from idleness, personifying an administrative form completely devoid of content.

Saakov was precisely such an administrator, existing by inertia, without any vital necessity. With a menacing, sullen look, threateningly moving his black waxed moustache, he walked the streets, but the police ruled here, leaving nothing for him, and he was simply not allowed into the Cheka, so as not to interfere. He was filled with administrative zeal and suffered unbearably from the impossibility of applying it, for he had neither subordinates nor wards; in addition, he belonged to that breed of people who regard any power that fell into their hands as a personal elevation above other mortals and the right to arbitrariness - in a word, he seemed to have moved to the new Soviet country from tsarist Russia, and even pre-reform. But he had nowhere to turn around, and he was forced to content himself with trifles - assault and extortion. Let the reader not be surprised that the enforcer and extortionist lived so long in Andijan: the people of those years still kept in their souls the oppression inherited from tsarism. In addition, Saakov did not fleece and beat everyone, but with a fine selection, so rumors of his exploits, if they reached the authorities, then indirectly and very unclearly. He was helped by some strong hand in Tashkent and an even more powerful hand in Moscow; he often hinted in conversations at his high connections. Only later did it become clear that in fact he had no connections either in Tashkent or in Moscow.

He chose a suburban flea market where they sold all sorts of old stuff as the place of his administrative activity. The police neglected the flea market and did not set up a post there. Saakov ruled here undividedly, everyone knew him, everyone was afraid of him, and no one thought of filing a complaint against him, the all-powerful and all-powerful one.

This continued until chance brought him together with Khalifa at a flea market. Saakov had just noticed a breach of order: old man Burygin, an elderly tsarist official, had brought out brass hunting cartridges for sale. In an old, faded official's cap with a velvet band that still bore the imprint of a cockade, with an unshaven chin and dull silver cheeks, Burygin was wandering around the bazaar, holding his goods, green with age, in the palm of his hand. The old man shuddered when Saakov suddenly appeared before him in his unchanging red riding breeches, a white Caucasian papakha, with a long, menacing moustache directed forward.

"Permission?" Saakov said menacingly, thinking back to the years gone by, when permission was indeed required to sell and buy hunting cartridges, which was intended to prevent the Basmachi from being supplied with ammunition. But those years were long gone, and Saakov remained, without having moved a single step forward toward a new life.

"Permission?" repeated Saakov. The old man squeaked weakly, crouched down and tried to slip away into the crowd.

- What? - thundered Saakov. - Run?! Run away from me?!

The old man dropped his shells and they rolled on the ground.

- Pick it up! Pick it up, I say!..

But the old man was so frightened that he did not understand anything and did not carry out the order; then Saakov grabbed him by the collar with his left hand and began to slap him on the cheeks with his right hand, saying:

- I'll teach you, I'll show you!..

Here someone suddenly hung on his arm, he roared in rage, turned around and saw Khalifa in front of him, pale, with burning eyes.

"Stop the beating!" she shouted commandingly. "You will be brought to trial!"

Saakov froze, froze for a second. But Khalifa was young and fragile in appearance, and he recovered.

"Who are you?" he wheezed, his eyes bulging and his face turning purple. "Where did you come from?"

"I am the people's judge Tashmukhamedova, and I hold you accountable for unlawful beating," Khalifa answered, but she did not have time to finish: her weak voice was drowned out by the mighty peals of Saakov's bass. He shouted, he threatened that he would hand over the trial to the court, that his basements in the commandant's office were full of such judges, and he shouted much more before he left with an angry step, trying to crush the ground with his boots as he went. His shouts were his last word. From then on, he was completely inaudible, and how he ended, I do not know. Khalifa became famous throughout Andijan after that.

I began to frequently attend court hearings that Khalifa was leading. One day, I met another acquaintance of mine, Alyoshka Konkin, among the defendants.

In court documents he was called citizen Aleksey Vladimirovich Konkin, but in life he was simply Alyoshka, which was more familiar and convenient for him.

He was a lively and quick-witted guy, but, unfortunately, a swindler. In addition, he was a skilled hunter, but even this noble passion lived in him, combined with an innate swindle. In Central Asia, duck and goose hunting is a winter time; one day in early December, Alyoshka went on a bicycle to the warm lakes for ducks. He shot the evening dawn, spent the night in a lakeside village with a farmer he knew, Akram-aki, hunted until dark the next day, and got ready to go home late in the evening. Winter evenings are dark, and the roads are bumpy and rutted, so before leaving, Alyoshka decided to light the bicycle carbide lantern and asked the owner for boiled water to charge it... And then Akram-aka saw something unusual: the water poured into the lantern's reservoir suddenly gave fire, and everything in front of the lantern was illuminated with an even and strong pale blue light.

"The water is burning!.. Is that possible?!" Akram-aka exclaimed in amazement, comparing the carbide lantern to a simple kerosene lamp.

Here Alyoshka should have explained to the man the difference between a lamp and a lantern, explained that it was not water that burned in the lantern, but acetylene gas, released by carbide under the influence of water, he should have taken a piece of carbide out of the lantern and shown it to Akram-aka, but Alyoshka was not like that: his selfish mind, always and unfailingly ready for deception, began to spin and work with incomprehensible speed.

"Yes," he answered. "It's an American lantern, you pour water into it instead of kerosene. And it burns, you see for yourself."

Akram-aka was amazed and silently contemplated the wonderful lantern. It must be said that kerosene was hard to come by in the villages, so they had to go to the city for kerosene. Akram-aka quickly realized what benefits this priceless lantern, in which simple water burned, could bring him.

"Sell it," he said to Alyoshka in a timid voice, confident in advance of a refusal, and indeed he received a refusal, but it sounded hesitant and not immediately, but after a short thought. "Aha, so it's a matter of price!" Akram-aka decided and persistently pestered Alyoshka with a request to sell. That was all he needed: after much squirming and being stubborn, he finally sold the lantern to Akram-aka for six chervonets - sixty rubles, that is, five times more than the store price.

He sold it and left. Akram-aka, despite the late hour, gathered his neighbors, and they sat for a long time, talking, marveling at the wonderful water lantern. At midnight, Akram-aka carefully put out the lantern, pouring out the water from it, the next evening he filled it again with boiled water, lit it again and again, having gathered his neighbors, enjoyed himself until midnight.

And on the third evening the lantern did not light. Akram-aka, worried, went to town with the lantern to Alyoshka, but did not find him at home and took the lantern to the bicycle repairman Teplyakov. The repairman replaced the carbide, the lantern lit up again; Akram-aka realized that he had been shamelessly deceived by Alyoshka, and on the advice of one chekaze, he filed a lawsuit. By the way, chekaze was not a nickname named after some insect, but a completely official title of a lawyer - a member of the college of defenders, just as the word "shkrab" did not mean a crustacean, but was the official title of a teacher - a school employee. Why it was necessary to change the familiar, understandable words "teacher" and "lawyer" to others, much less euphonious, I do not know, perhaps it was a tribute to the whirlwind of general changes sweeping over the country at that time.

So, Akram-aka filed a lawsuit against Alyoshka, and it was precisely this case that Khalifa had to deal with. The assessors were the cotton-ginning plant mechanic Mosin and the railway weigher Pozdnyakov. Alyoshka behaved impudently in court and immediately challenged Khalifa on the grounds that she was Uzbek and would indulge her own, that is, Akram-aka. The court conferred in whispers, and Khalifa, turning pale, announced the decision - to reject the challenge as unfounded.

"National identity is not taken into account by the Soviet court," she explained. "Besides, both people's assessors are Russian."

"They're both like stumps in the forest, they don't understand anything," Alyoshka responded.

Then the weigher Pozdnyakov, an elderly man and highly respected by all, said, turning pale:

- Don't talk, Alyoshka!

- Defendant citizen Konkin Aleksey Vladimirovich, the court asks you to choose your words, otherwise the court will fine you or even arrest you, - Khalifa announced. - What else do you have to say to the court at the beginning of the hearing?

Alyoshka waved his hand and sat down. The floor was given to Akram-aka, he told everything as it happened. Alyoshka began to squirm, to dodge, saying that he had correctly explained to Akram-aka the structure of the carbide lantern and had not called it a water lantern at all, that Akram-aka, in his ignorance, simply had not understood him.

"How much did you pay for this lantern at the store?" Khalifa asked.

- Twelve roubles.

— And you sold it for sixty?

"I didn't force him to pay," snapped Alyoshka, "I didn't pick his pocket."

"We are not trying you for pickpocketing, but for fraud," Khalifa answered calmly. "Such and such an article of the Criminal Code provides for imprisonment for a term of three months to two years for fraud."

Alyoshka looked back at the audience, his eyes became round, and he no longer entered into an argument with Khalifa.

The court retired to deliberate.

The sentence announced by Khalifa was unexpectedly lenient: Alyoshka was sentenced to return sixty rubles to Akram-ake and to reimburse legal costs, that's all.

But, reading the sentence, Khalifa suddenly faltered at the last lines, turned pale... she finished reading with difficulty and immediately went into the deliberation room. Alyoshka's friends rushed to him - some, the smarter ones, to congratulate him, others, the stupider ones, to sympathize. Suddenly the door of the deliberation room opened, the weigher Pozdnyakov appeared on the threshold and shouted into the hall:

- Water! Hurry!

Khalifa needed water: having finished the case, she felt ill. There is nothing surprising in this, if you think that she was the first female judge in Uzbekistan and held in her hands the fates of others, while three years ago she was not the mistress of her own fate and lived locked up under a black blanket - her transition from complete lack of rights to full rights and even to the guardianship of this right was too steep, she still had to get used to the new situation.

A woman judge - this will not surprise anyone today. But how excitedly the whole of Andijan buzzed when a new people's judge Khalifa Tashmu-khammedova appeared in the city.

Her story is common for those times, fantastic for today. Let's start in the language of those times: the average price of an average girl was 6 horses, 2 cows, 10 rams and 300 rubles in money, which means about 1200 rubles in total. The same was the cost of a three-year-old horse of the purebred Akhal-Teke breed; if it was of a rare color, for example, gray with apples, its price increased to 1500 rubles. The price of the girl also increased in accordance with her beauty.

For Khalifa Tashmukhamedova, the father received 10 horses, 6 cows, 30 rams and 800 rubles in money, from which it is clear that Khalifa was a girl of dazzling beauty.

Young husbands tend to boast about their wives' beauty, which often leads to undesirable consequences. The Uzbeks, having overcome the temptation of vanity, wisely hid their wives under chachvans - black nets made of horsehair, but the revolution came, brought a new way of life, the women rebelled, the chachvans flew into the fire. Khalifa's chachvan also flew - into the fire lit by the Komsomol members on the main city square of Andijan.

By what means did news of the new life penetrate, news from the outside to it, into the deaf, stuffy ichkari - the women's half of the house? It must have been brought by old women who peddled women's trifles. Conversations about the new life were conducted in the ichkari, of course condemnatory, with a sanctimonious pursing of the lips, and Khalifa listened to these conversations as if they were laudatory, and more and more often she was overcome by a sinful, impudent thought - to violate, to destroy the law of the past, to throw off the chachvan, to leave the ichkari for freedom, for the sun.

Much has been written and is still being written abroad about the purely Russian, nationally limited character of our revolution. This view of the October Revolution is flawed at its core.

Why did the revolution triumph so confidently in all corners and nooks of Russia? Why did it triumph in Turkestan, a remote and not at all Russian country, with a different history and a different way of life? There is no point in talking about direct violence here - during the civil war, Turkestan, located three thousand kilometers from the center and connected to Russia by a single railroad thread, could have separated from Russia ten times without hindrance, especially since there were only two hundred thousand Russians there out of fifteen million locals, that is, one Russian for seventy-five locals. It would have been easy to expel all the Russians, but they did not expel them, they did not even feud with the Russians, as, say, the Algerians are feuding with the French, the Angolese with the Portuguese. There is only one reason for such peacefulness of the Uzbeks, a generally warlike and freedom-loving people - the Russians did not deserve to be expelled, since the spirit of national arrogance was alien to them. The Russians, oppressed and crushed by tsarism, understood the Uzbeks, sympathized with them, the Uzbeks understood the Russians, and with mutual understanding, hostility becomes impossible. The colonial policy of tsarism was, like any colonial policy, both harsh and cruel, but the Russian national character introduced into this policy a significant amendment for equality, the very one that neither the French nor the English introduced. After the revolution, Turkestan did not separate, did not break the alliance with the new Russia, on the contrary, it strengthened and consolidated this alliance in the name of its future; today's Uzbekistan, Tajikistan, Turkmenistan, Kazakhstan and Kyrgyzstan - the most advanced countries of modern Asia - are the best proof of the correctness of the path they chose together with Russia.

My reasoning may seem naive, but I am convinced that it was precisely the peculiarities of the Russian national character that in many ways, very much, determined the victory of the October Revolution, all our subsequent victories, and continue to determine them.

...Khalifa Tashmukhamedova, one of millions of people living on earth, heard the call of a new life. Without consulting anyone, she prepared her rebellion against the ossified past alone, found herself on the due day in the square in front of the fire, and revealed her face to the Komsomol members. "Rakhmat, yashasun!" the Komsomol members shouted. She threw the chachvan into the fire - from now on all paths back to the old life were cut off for her.

Two days later, she was taken to the hospital with a deep knife wound under her left breast. The knife was the usual response to women's urges for freedom in those days. Murderers were caught, tried, shot, but it took years before the old law was reconciled and retreated. Khalifa was treated, sent to Tashkent to study; three years later, she returned to her native Andijan as a party member and a people's judge.

I was very interested in the fate of the young Uzbek woman; working as a "journalist" on incoming and outgoing lines, I did not give up hope of becoming a real journalist and writing the story of Khalifa.

Meanwhile, winter was leaving, cool days were replaced by warm days of spring rains, and the irrigation ditches were filling with water.

But then the rains stopped, and the roads and gardens began to dry out under the hot sun. The air was filled with the scent of young leaves. I couldn't sit in the stuffy court office. The road beckoned me again.

Over the winter I saved enough money to buy a train ticket to the city I was going to and to survive for a while until I got a job. But where to go?!

My father, sending me off in the German manner, to all four sides, wanted me to learn about life and feed myself.

I thought I had learned life and had provided for myself. I could have gone home, but I remembered my conversation with my father, his dismissive attitude toward my writing inclinations, and I did not want to go home.

The desire to write flared up again in me, stifled by years of my wandering. I remembered the signature "Awake". It made me laugh. No, now I would not sign it that way and I would write not fantastic stories, but about real life, big, multifaceted, seen with my own eyes.

I resigned from the court and bought a ticket to Tashkent.
1960–1961

[66000 words]

www.ingramcontent.com/pod-product-compliance
Lightning Source LLC
LaVergne TN
LVHW011233080426
835509LV00005B/468